TRUMAN'S WHISTLE-STOP CAMPAIGN

Library of Presidential Rhetoric

Truman's Whistle-Stop Campaign

Steven R. Goldzwig

Texas A&M University Press : College Station

Frontispiece: Harry S. Truman greeting the public during his whistle-stop tour, 1948. Photograph by Abbie Rowe, National Park Service, courtesy Harry S. Truman Library.

This paper meets the requirements
of ANSI/NISO Z39.48–1992 (Permanence of Paper)
Binding materials have been chosen for durability.

Library of Congress Cataloging-in-Publication Data

Goldzwig, Steven R.
Truman's whistle-stop campaign / Steven R. Goldzwig. — 1st ed.
p. cm. — (Library of presidential rhetoric)
Includes bibliographical references and index.
ISBN-13: 978-1-60344-005-9 (cloth : alk. paper)
ISBN-10: 1-60344-005-4 (cloth : alk. paper)
ISBN-13: 978-1-60344-006-6 (pbk. : alk. paper)
ISBN-10: 1-60344-006-2 (pbk. : alk. paper)
1. Truman, Harry S., 1884–1972.   2. Truman, Harry S.,
1884–1972—Oratory.   3. Presidents—United States—Election—1948.
4. Presidential candidates—United States—Biography.
5. Political oratory—United States—History—20th century.
6. Rhetoric—Political aspects—United States—History—20th century.
7. Political campaigns—United States—History—20th century.
8. United States—Politics and government—1945–1953.
9. Presidents—United States—Biography.   I. Title.
E815.G64   2008
324.973'0918—dc22
2007026473

Contents

Acknowledgments

Writing a book accrues indebtedness. This project is no exception. I would like to thank the Harry S. Truman Library Institute for a research travel grant that was instrumental in the completion of this study. I am grateful to the Graduate Committee of the J. William and Mary Diederich College of Communication and the Committee on Research at Marquette University for their generous support.

I also would like to thank the wonderful archival staff of the Truman Library, whose able assistance proved invaluable during my several trips to Independence, Missouri. In particular, I am grateful for the inimitable and indomitable Liz Safly, the voluminous knowledge of Dennis Bilger, and the competent and cheerful service of other stalwarts, including Randy Sowell, David Clark, and Pauline Testerman. Each of these individuals made my work in the Truman Library research room a rewarding and delightful experience.

I am especially indebted to Martin J. Medhurst for his steadfast encouragement and advice on this project. Marty has been instrumental in advancing my scholarship many times over the years. Rhetorical studies as a discipline has benefited immensely from Marty's meticulous, visionary stewardship.

Finally, I thank Mary Lenn Dixon, Texas A&M University Press; the Library of Presidential Rhetoric advisory board; Tiff Pua, who proofread the original manuscript and assisted in the completion of the initial editing; Will Gartside for his invaluable assistance with the index; Mia Scroggs for final copyediting; and my anonymous external reviewers for their help toward the completion of this study.

Introduction

While a number of books have been written on the 1948 campaign for the presidency, none has yet fully accounted for the rhetorical importance of Harry S. Truman's whistle-stop train tour during that remarkable campaign. An analysis focusing on the president's major campaign speeches and whistle-stop remarks resurrects an older period in our modern political history by providing a narrative account of Harry S. Truman's memorable stops at countless cities, towns, and villages across an expansive national territory in pursuit of an election most thought beyond the president's grasp. This book will furnish a rationale for why Truman undertook the strenuous trip and is intended to lend additional insight into presidential stump speaking in the conduct of a national presidential campaign. In addition, this study seeks a clear interpretation and evaluation of Truman's rhetorical efforts as he barnstormed the country by rail. It will be argued that Truman's attempts at rhetorical influence were key factors in his startling upset victory over Thomas E. Dewey.

In particular, this study will advance the claim that Truman's rhetorical campaign was largely a "populist" effort to build a political coalition of laborers, farmers, and African Americans (along with secondary appeals to small business owners and consumers pestered by inflation) to consolidate key blocs of voters crucial to the November election. These key groups were also most susceptible to and largely identified with Truman's populist persuasive appeals. The president's populist rhetorical style was perfectly suited to the man, his public policy initiatives, and the times.

The bulk of this study will center on the major speeches and the back-platform remarks. Each is an important rhetorical form and each deserves further study. The major speeches played a pivotal role in establishing the overall agenda and sustained key themes and issues throughout the campaign while the whistle-stop remarks highlighted the themes and issues established in the major speeches as they applied to a particular region or locality. Unlike most of the major speeches, train-side talks were largely delivered extemporaneously. Back-platform remarks also allowed Truman to highlight a major speech that had either already been delivered or was significant enough to invite those standing trackside to attend in the near future. A focus on both the major speeches *and* the whistle-stop back-platform remarks will help sustain a more complete rhetorical analysis and a more vivid image of a candidate involved in a well-planned and complicated presidential campaign. As George M. Elsey, one of the principal whistle-stop speechwriters who accompanied President Truman on the campaign train, has observed, the "unforeseen victory in '48 was no accident. It resulted from thoughtful planning, bold actions, and an acute reading of the voters' minds."[1]

As everyone knows, this is the story of a president who was given little chance of winning the 1948 election. President Truman made it his task to demonstrate to pundits, pollsters, politicians, and other assorted naysayers that he could win an election in his own right by trusting the wisdom of the people. Traveling the nation by rail, Truman used his amazing energy and homespun charm to counter negative images and reveal his unique character as he conducted a vigorous national campaign to win the hearts and minds of voters. Displaying unrivaled persistence and stamina, the president employed a series of major addresses and back-platform remarks at the whistle-stops of a diverse nation to define the issues, articulate the stakes, and bring home an unexpected election victory. Truman appealed to America and America responded. A rhetorical interpretation of Truman's public address during that transitional campaign will shed additional light on a uniquely American political narrative well worth preserving.

TRUMAN'S WHISTLE-STOP CAMPAIGN

Text of Harry S. Truman's Rear-Platform Remarks in Decatur, Illinois, October 12, 1948

Mr. Chairman, my fellow Democrats of Decatur:

I appreciate most highly this cordial welcome. You know, when I first started out on these tours, I made an effort to estimate the crowds, and I found that I just couldn't estimate them at all—and found I had to measure them by the acre. I did some figuring, and I figured out that in an acre, there are 4,850 square yards and that there ought to be at least two people to the square yard, and when you have an acre of people, you have 9,600 people, and when you have ten acres of people, you have 96,000. Now, I would say that we might have about five acres of people here this afternoon—and I can't tell you how much I appreciate it. It shows that you are interested in this campaign. It shows that you are interested in the welfare of the country, and I appreciate it. And I am always happy to see the young people come out because they are going to have the responsibility of running this country in the next generation. And they ought to be interested and they ought to understand all the issues that are before the country now.

I want to compliment these Junior Police for coming out and helping to preserve order this afternoon. They are doing a good job. This is one of the most orderly crowds I have seen.

The kind of receptions I have been getting here in Illinois today mean you are vitally concerned with what is going on in the country. It means that you are going to send Paul Douglas to the Senate, and Olive Remington Goldman to the House of Representatives, and Adlai Stevenson to the state capitol in Springfield.

Now, I have been making a crusade all over this country to tell the American people what the issues in this campaign are. I am explaining just exactly what this election means to them. The Republicans are trying to pretend that there aren't any issues. Well, they couldn't be further from the truth if they tried, and they don't stick very closely to the truth very often.

This election will decide who runs the government of the United States for the next four years. It will decide whether you, the people, are in control or whether a little group of reactionary Republicans, completely under the thumb of the lobbies of the special interests, will be in office and run the country.

I want to say to you that this 80th Congress was beset with more lobbyists than any other Congress in the history of the country, and they spent more money than ever has been spent in Washington in lobbies in the history of the country—and that Congress did nothing about it. They liked it. They sat and took it.

I have been going around the country, explaining how the actions of the Republican 80th Congress, which the Republican candidate for president has warmly endorsed, undermined the very foundation of the prosperity of the American people as they are enjoying it now.

In 1933, after twelve years of Republican misrule, Decatur was in very serious trouble. I am sure you remember what it was like in the railroad shops and the mills and plants and all the stores and shops that supply the farmers in this part of Illinois. Well, you got sort of tired of that, and in 1932 you elected Franklin D. Roosevelt president of the United States.

There was a steady improvement from that time on. And the postwar years have brought the greatest prosperity this area has ever known. That wasn't by accident. That came about because the Democratic Party believes in seeing that labor gets its fair share of the national income and that the farmer is on a parity basis with the rest of the economy, and that the small businessmen get a square deal. The Democrats passed the Wagner Act and the Fair Labor Standards Act and the Social Security Act and a great many other measures that give workers better incomes and greater security than they ever had before in the history of the country. We provided for soil conservation and rural electrification and the farm price support program and a number of other laws—all to help the farmer, the workingman, and the small businessman. When the farmers and the workers are well off, then the businessmen are able to do well.

Since we are enjoying our present great prosperity, why can't it just continue on like this? We can't count on continued prosperity going on just like this because we have so many serious problems that need action, and they need action now. I tried all through the 80th Congress to get the Republican leaders to act on the worst problem of all—high prices. If this runaway inflation is not stopped, we are surely headed straight for another bust. But the Republican leaders absolutely refused to take one step that would bring down the cost of living. They refused to pass any housing bill which would clear away the city slums, provide public low-rental housing, or help meet the acute housing shortage in the rural areas. They refused to do anything about the crisis in education, or to help meet the acute shortage of doctors and hospitals, or to build the waterways and dams and power plants we need if we are to continue to grow. The Republican 80th Congress not only refused to meet our pressing national problems, they actually tried to tear down the Democratic programs which are responsible for the growth and prosperity of this great country for the past 16 years.

Last night in Akron, Ohio, I told how the Republicans tried to crush the strength of the labor movement, how they took away social security from nearly a million people, how they have plans to take away even more of the rights of the workingman if they ever get a chance.

Tonight in Springfield, Illinois, I am going to tell just exactly what the Republicans have done to the farmers—how they have already deprived many farmers of price supports, how they have cut rural electrification and soil conservation funds, how they have tried to put the farmer back where he was in the 1920s.

Remember, all these actions of the Republican 80th "do-nothing" Congress were approved by the Republican candidate for president when he said, "the 80th Congress delivered as no other Congress has done for the future of the country."

By your vote on November 2nd you can get a government that's not going to forget about you in Washington. You are going to get a government that will work for the welfare of the people—if you vote right. But you can get a government on November 2d that will forget about you in Washington and worry only about the interests of big business—you can get a Republican government, which would be the worst thing that could happen to this country at this time.

I hope that you will make the right choice and that you'll have a government that has the interests of the people at heart, a government headed by Democrats—who believe in Democratic principles, who believe in the welfare of the whole country, and not just in the welfare of a special few.

I ask you to look at the record. Then get your friends and neighbors to get to the polls on election day, November the 2nd. And just keep this in mind: When you go there, vote for yourselves; vote in your own interest. When you do that, you'll vote a straight Democratic ticket—and you'll have a Democratic governor in Springfield, you'll have a Democratic Senator from Illinois, you'll have a Democratic Congressman from this district, and you'll have a Democratic president in the White House—and then I won't be troubled with the housing shortage next January.

I can't tell you how much I appreciate this interest and this turnout. It is magnificent. You can't appreciate it unless you can stand up here and look at all these smiling faces showing all the interest in the things that are taking place.[1]

Setting the Political and Rhetorical Strategy, January–May 1948

In 1945, American servicemen were returning home and looking to make a new life for themselves in the hoped-for prosperity brought by peace. The peacetime conversion, however, was still nascent and struggling; many crucial moves had yet to be accomplished. As the 1946 midterm elections approached, a host of intractable problems darkened the national mood. Internationally, Communist Russia loomed as an emerging threat. Domestically, industries needed to be retooled, new housing had to be constructed, consumer products were often in short supply, inflation was too high, there were complaints of government corruption and mismanagement, and labor union unrest in the rail and steel industries conspired to diminish the national sense of security and prosperity. The president had little luck passing legislation on a host of issues, including social security, housing, poll taxes, anti-lynching laws, fair employment provisions, and anti-inflation efforts. As columnist Walter Lippmann warned, "At the very center of the Truman administration . . . there is a vacuum of responsibility and authority."[1] Many simply believed that the president was unable to lead the nation and support Americans as they fulfilled their sky-high expectations. As one scholar noted, "High priced scarcity was no recipe for electoral success."[2]

In October of 1946, less than a month before the national midterm elections, presidential administrative assistant David K. Niles warned Truman's appointments secretary, Matthew Connelly, "Gallup's report will indicate that never since they have been taking polls has there been such a swing away from the Administration as has been taking place the past six weeks. In their opinion the Senate and the House will both go Republican." Niles described growing concerns over housing, strikes, government expenses, the Russian threat, and the cost of living.[3]

Many Democrats facing reelection in 1946, therefore, were quite wary of sharing the stage with Truman, whose public stumbling was becoming a political embarrassment. The 1946 midterm elections reflected the national discontent. Democrats would have to contend with Republican majorities in both the House (245–188) and the Senate (55–40). Two years later, the Republican-dominated Eightieth Congress kept a variety of bills tied up in committee that had particular implications for social welfare, including initiatives directed at housing, health care, an increase in the minimum wage, fair employment practices, and displaced persons legislation, among others. The president seemed powerless to break the logjam.

Many Democrats were beginning to feel the need to recruit a new presidential candidate for 1948. One Truman loyalist wrote the president to express his dismay over what appeared to be a "national stampede, gathering dangerous and revolutionary momentum" to "drive you from the White House." The off-year election returns coupled with the hue and cry raised by members of the press had greatly distressed this self-identified "true blue" Democrat. Truman remained unflappable. His prior political experience and judgment suggested to him that he could weather the storm. Truman had survived a number of close political battles, not the least of which was his hotly contested 1940 campaign for the U.S. Senate. In characteristically sanguine terms, Truman replied, "I think you are unduly alarmed at a situation that develops frequently in our political set up and it doesn't worry me a great deal."[4]

Despite such optimism, as the 1948 election approached the president was up against some rather ominous political developments. There was a growing draft-Eisenhower movement within the Democratic

Party, an impending Dixiecrat rebellion, and an additional challenge posed by Henry Wallace's leftist Progressive Party. Organized labor, the liberal Americans for Democratic Action (ADA), and the local and state Democratic leaders also demonstrated little confidence in the president.[5] Truman would be forced not only to deal with the typical Republican challenges posed by the upcoming 1948 campaign but also straddle and defend simultaneously attacks from his own party regulars, conservatives in the South who rejected his civil rights proposals, and progressives in the North who objected to what they viewed as the president's hardline and counterproductive anticommunism. Thus, Truman's leadership was challenged by a formidable host of powerful forces. All too aware of the challenges ahead, the president and his advisers began preparing for the upcoming campaign. A political and a rhetorical strategy had to be developed, honed, and executed.

1948 Campaign Strategy

The 1948 campaign strategy was largely laid down in the famous memorandum written by attorney and New Dealer James H. Rowe titled "The Politics of 1948." In this thirty-three-page document, later expanded to forty-three pages and sent to the president by Special Counsel Clark Clifford, Rowe outlined his "basic premise" that "the Democratic Party is an unhappy alliance of Southern conservatives, Western progressives, and Big City Labor." The goal of the campaign was to "lead enough members of these three misfit groups to the polls on the first Tuesday after the first Monday of November, 1948." The memo predicted that Thomas Dewey would be nominated as the Republican presidential candidate and that Henry Wallace would mount a third-party bid. For the president to win the election, he had to rely on the traditional Democratic alliances, especially in the South and the West. Indicating (somewhat inaccurately and prematurely given the Dixiecrat revolt that would follow) that the South was "safely Democratic," Rowe advised focusing on "the West and its problems." The "independent and progressive voter[s]" held "the balance of power in 1948," but their support would not be won without "great effort." To secure victory, the president had to direct his campaign appeals to key interest groups. Among the groups identified as crucial to building a winning coalition that would put the president over the top were farmers, labor, liberals and progressives, and African Americans. These groups were to be specifically targeted, and none of them could be taken for granted. While farmers would be particularly important in delivering votes from the West, African Americans could tip the balance in the North. Indeed, the memo highlighted the potentially critical importance of African Americans in the election outcome: "A theory of professional politicians is that the northern Negro voter today holds the balance of power in Presidential elections for the simple arithmetical reason that the Negroes not only vote in a bloc but are geographically concentrated in the pivotal, large, and closely contested electoral states such as New York, Illinois, Pennsylvania, Ohio and Michigan. This theory may or may not be absolutely true, but it is certainly close enough to the truth to be extremely arguable."

The general domestic election strategies also could be buttressed by direct confrontation with the Soviet Union. Truman's hardline stance was certainly drawn from personal convictions, but it had added benefits in winning over the electorate. As this famous campaign memo indicates, "There is considerable political advantage to the Administration in its battle with the Kremlin." Simply put: "In times of crisis the American citizen tends to back up his President."[6]

As the campaign drew near, Clifford sent the president another memo that further delineated its main objectives. First, there should be an attempt to sustain the fifteen million independent voters who voted for the Democratic Party in the four previous elections. A primary way to do that would be to attack the Eightieth Congress, implicate Dewey in its poor performance and inaction, and then rally the citizenry behind the Democratic Party's New Deal social programs, emphasizing concrete progress and a better future. Second, it was imperative that election strategies and appeals be targeted toward those who were "predominately" key Democratic Party supporters: "workers, veterans, and Negroes." The memo also cautioned that "farmers, small businessmen, and other groups" could not be overlooked. Finally, while domestic issues seemed to predominate, relations with the Soviets were tenuous at best; people were fearful of deteriorating circumstances that might lead to another war. It was argued that the best way to position international affairs was to stay the course and to demonstrate conclusively that "the president's policy has kept the Nation on a road leading to peace, and that change in this policy may lead to war."

Clifford also commented on how these campaign objectives were perhaps best realized. On the domestic front, winning the independent liberal vote would mean gathering the support of the principal labor unions and other liberal groups. And "by hammering away on the failures of the 80th Congress, the President can show the people what to expect from the Republicans." In appealing to workers, the president was advised to demand the repeal of the Taft-Hartley Act, call attention to his "fine record" on labor, hit upon Republican failures in restoring price controls, and tar them with "ineffective" anti-inflation measures. Appeals to veterans should highlight the president's "combat service," his "clear recognition of the needs of veterans," and the benefits of the G.I. Bill. Finally, in framing his appeals to African Americans, the president was advised to "speak out fully on his Civil Rights record." That record included past votes in the Senate, support for the wartime Fair Employment Practices Committee, and his recent executive orders on ending discrimination in the federal government and the armed forces of the United States. Truman was counseled to emphasize that his "record proves that he acts as well as talks Civil Rights." From a political standpoint, it was assumed that "the Negro votes in the crucial states will more than cancel out any votes the President may lose in the South."

Internationally, the advice was for the president to "reiterate constantly that he has directed our foreign policy with the purpose of establishing not merely peace in our time but peace for all time." A good tack would be to argue that the Truman Doctrine and the European Recovery Program were bulwarks for "maintaining the integrity of free states against Communist pressure." It was suggested that Truman's best rhetorical and political strategy was to ask Americans to support his established foreign policy.

Finally, the memo proposed that the president focus his campaign energies on the seventeen states "which went to one party or another by very narrow margins in 1944." These included the New England states of New Hampshire, Massachusetts, and Connecticut; the Mid-Atlantic states of New York, New Jersey, Pennsylvania, and Maryland; the Midwest states of Ohio, Indiana, Illinois, Michigan, Wisconsin, Minnesota, Iowa, and Truman's own home state of Missouri; and the mountain states of Idaho and Wyoming. The president was advised to spend "a large part of his time in [these] critical states." He also was cautioned to "make his major speeches in the 23 largest city-county areas." Those areas represented the greatest number of industrial workers and low-income families, two major constituencies that had given FDR "overwhelming majorities" and "in most instances, were decisive in swinging the electoral votes of their states." The fall campaign train itinerary would ultimately reflect these suggestions almost verbatim. It was recommended that the president focus on a tour of the Midwest, the West, and the eastern United States. Some consideration was also given to a brief tour of the South.[7]

In sum, domestic policy seemed to be privileged over foreign policy in planning key issues for the upcoming campaign. Truman had called for and largely received cooperation in a "bi-partisan" approach in international affairs with the rationale that domestic politics should stop at the water's edge.[8] Nevertheless, foreign policy would intervene to some degree as unfolding events in world capitals continued to beg for strong, clear responses. For instance, in mid-March of 1948, the Soviets staged a coup in Czechoslovakia; for Truman, this made the adoption of the Marshall Plan that much more urgent. In mid-May the president recognized the new state of Israel. In June and July, the Berlin blockade was heating up. These international affairs and occasional flare-ups required a well-timed rhetorical response, if only to dissipate growing national trepidation. Advisers counseled vigorous leadership in foreign affairs as a necessary component of the upcoming campaign.[9] Even so, the importance of foreign policy in the 1948 campaign has often been overlooked.[10] In particular, Harry Truman addressed the national fear of war on a number of occasions during the campaign, and analysis of a selected sample of such instances is therefore both warrantable and necessary.

Speech Strategy for the Campaign

Along with the political planning, a general rhetorical strategy had to be developed. In an unsigned and undated memorandum we encounter "suggestions for presidential speeches in an election year." The directive is consonant with what the president actually did try to accomplish during the campaign. The memo advised the president to adopt a "prophetic, personal voice." It said that the best approach was to treat "basic issues" in the form of a "*person-to-person* talk" (emphasis original). It emphasized that the "average fellow" really "wants to know what is going to happen to him and his family" and because he was "exceptionally good at political intuition," he would "accept the challenge of a fellow believer and fellow citizen" like Truman. The trick was to address "one thing at one time." Also, since "the basic issues are *great* issues, they can be told in monosyllabic language." While the president certainly had to attack the campaign trail in an all-out effort to put "the Republicans and the Wallaceites on the defensive and *keep* them there," it was also necessary for the rhetoric driving the politics in 1948 to be more than merely strategic: "This is a time for *spiritual* greatness, so please remember that the average citizen hungers for true courage and political statesmanship."[11] This latter point was open to some question since it was not entirely clear that Truman had such inspirational rhetorical capabilities.

Even if the president were to develop additional rhetorical prowess, many people still considered Truman unelectable. They simply felt he was neither smart enough nor experienced enough to protect and defend the free world. Placed in the presidency by fate, many people seemed convinced fate would be his undoing. One campaign billboard that appeared prior to the nominating conventions in Tulsa, Oklahoma, summarized Truman's predicament well: "Truman said he wasn't big enough to be

President—and he ain't. Vote Republican in '48."[12] Truman would have to work hard to overcome that kind of sentiment—and work he did.

Undeterred by the low poll numbers and the increasing disdain for his governance, Truman employed his January State of the Union address to inaugurate his well-formulated 1948 campaign strategy. According to George M. Elsey, the message "was deliberately written so that it could be translated into the Democratic platform. Among other things, [the president] asked for civil rights, for broader social security, for federal aid for housing and education, and for higher minimum wages." Each of these measures pressed for legislation that ordinary citizens and minorities could appreciate, and each supported the interests of the coalition Truman was trying to patch together for the upcoming election. His attack on the Republican-dominated Eightieth Congress would be premised on legislative proposals that seemed certain to be rejected. As Elsey also indicated, "The President had little hope that any of these measures would be passed by the 80th Congress although he was convinced that they were favored by the American people."[13]

In highlighting policy issues critical to the "common man," Truman underscored his continued commitment to FDR's New Deal tradition. Truman's prescriptions were wedded both to the principles of the Democratic Party and to the populist aspirations the president would invoke in his upcoming campaign. Dewey was cast in the role of aristocratic frontrunner; Truman as underdog would comfortably play the role of "man of the people" by linking his common roots to common sense, trusting that the people would respond favorably. Though he had not yet declared his candidacy, Truman's State of the Union message unveiled his apparent desire to run for the presidency in his own right. "His laundry list of improbable proposals previewed his platform, seized the initiative, and threw down the gauntlet," according to Gullan.[14]

The pledge to send Congress civil rights legislation was particularly vexing for southern Democrats and threatened to split the party. But Truman needed the votes of African Americans, a constituency that could exercise a number of options in the 1948 election. Both Thomas E.

Dewey and Henry A. Wallace strongly supported civil rights. Approximately one week after the State of the Union message, the president's speechwriters began working on a draft of a civil rights speech for delivery before a joint session of Congress.

Building an African American voter base in the 1940s was an intriguing and rather complex operation. The African American vote was necessary to the president's electoral success, but numerous instances of postwar discrimination and violent mistreatment continued to hinder domestic tranquility and test the president's resolve. African Americans put pressure on the president to protect and extend their civil rights. The president took this divisive issue on as both a personal cause and a constitutional duty.

Relations with the African American community also had international repercussions. In the new post–World War II environment, the United States had signed the U.N. Charter on Human Rights, and it was imperative that the United States be viewed by all nations as upholding human rights in practice as well as principle. The unfair treatment of African Americans was an item that could be exploited by Soviet propaganda, and it threatened to weaken the case for democracy worldwide.

On December 5, 1946, Truman signed Executive Order 9808, which appointed a committee to report directly to him on civil rights. The president told the newly assembled President's Committee on Civil Rights pointedly and concisely, "I want our Bill of Rights implemented in fact. We have been trying to do this for 150 years. We are making progress, but we are not making progress fast enough."[15]

Truman addressed the matter of civil rights personally in his memorable and groundbreaking June 29, 1947, address to the NAACP. As McCoy and Ruetten observe, "the message represented a clear-cut victory for advocates of racial justice in America" because it "clearly foreshadowed an assault on segregation everywhere in America."[16]

Two key themes emerged from that speech that would have consequences for the 1948 campaign. First, the president maintained that domestic civil rights abuses had to be solved and quickly: "Our immediate task," a forceful president declared, "is to remove the last remnants of the barriers which stand between millions of our citizens and their birthright. There is no justifiable reason for discrimination because of ancestry, or religion, or race, or color." The United States "could no longer afford a leisurely attack upon prejudice and discrimination." His sense of urgency was palpable and unprecedented.

Second, this imperative stemmed not only from Truman's genuine concern for ameliorating an intractable and often viciously violent problem but also from ongoing reports that racial unrest and violence was becoming an international embarrassment. As the president acknowledged, "Freedom is not an easy lesson to teach, nor an easy cause to sell, to peoples beset by every kind of privation. They may surrender to the false security offered so temptingly by totalitarian regimes unless we can prove the superiority of democracy. Our case for democracy should be as strong as we can make it."[17] As one state department official observed, the suppression of human rights in the United States was a source of outrage in the international community, "destroy[ing] the idea of the United States as the land of freedom," and perhaps, even more importantly, diminishing credibility on the issue "since the continued existence of totalitarian regimes depends upon the suppression of human rights." Truman was at the helm of an evolving Cold War ideology bent on persuading various nation-states that the United States was best equipped to guarantee human rights; this was labeled "the central issue of present-day world politics."[18] Civil rights abuses, then, tarnished America's own self-image and its image in the international community; the disposition of civil rights in the United States therefore became a particularly difficult and testy political issue with both national and international implications.[19]

The centrality of the civil rights issue was underscored once again when the President's Committee on Civil Rights delivered its final report October 29, 1947. Truman told the committee that he was hopeful that their report be recognized widely as "an American charter of human freedom in our time." He expected the report to serve as a "guide for action" on behalf of civil rights in the United States and just as importantly, that "in the eyes of the world" the finished document would be regarded as "a declaration of our renewed faith in the American goal—the integrity of the individual human being, sustained by the moral consensus of the whole nation, protected by a government based on equal freedom under just laws."[20] The committee's comprehensive and progressive work would serve the president and the nation well for the next half century.[21]

On February 2, 1948, Truman delivered on his promise to introduce civil rights legislation. Fashioning his legislative agenda from recommendations made by his civil rights committee, the president anticipated that political and practical necessities were against him. While the chances of getting this controversial package though Congress seemed slim, the attempt was premised on both political need and personal conviction.

Truman grounded his remarks in traditional constitutional principles and democratic ideals, which included the firm belief that "all men are created equal and that they have the right to equal justice under law." However, not all Americans enjoyed justice and realized equal opportunity and, sadly, not all Americans were interested in preserving them for their fellow citizens. Truman told Congress that his civil rights committee had uncovered conditions that now seemed embarrassingly obvious: "[T]here is a serious gap between our ideals and some of our practices. This gap must be closed."

Given this rationale, the president proposed ten recommendations, including the establishment of a permanent Commission on Civil Rights; the strengthening of existing civil rights statutes; federal protections against lynching; voting rights protections; a Fair Employment Practices Commission; prohibition of discrimination in interstate transportation facilities; and provision of home-rule and suffrage in presidential elections for the residents of the District of Columbia. Asking Congress to enact these measures "at the present session," Truman described his initiatives as "a minimum program if the Federal Government is to fulfill its obligation of insuring the Constitutional guarantees of individual liberties and of equal protection under the law." The president also promised executive action to combat discrimination in federal employment and the armed forces. Truman concluded his address with a reference to the international implications of his civil rights legislation, indicating that the path was now clear to achieve justice, ensure domestic tranquility, and gain worldwide acclaim: "If we wish to inspire the peoples of the world whose freedom is in jeopardy, if we wish to restore hope to those who have already lost their civil liberties, if we wish to fulfill the promise that is ours, we must correct the remaining imperfections in our practice of democracy. We know the way. We need only the will."[22]

Many felt Truman was going too far, too fast. Some felt that by calling for so many measures at once, Truman's political strategy was sure to fail. Others, especially from the South, were simply outraged at the introduction of any civil rights initiative. One thing was certain: for the first time in history, a president had delivered a special message to Congress on civil rights. In garnering overwhelming African American approval for these efforts, Truman had also shored up a key constituency for the upcoming campaign.

On March 8, 1948, Democratic National Committee Chair Senator J. Howard McGrath announced that Truman would indeed stand for election in his own right; concurrently, it was reported that the president intended to press his civil rights legislation. This was interpreted as a signal that Truman would not kowtow to the powerful Democrats in the South. Truman's willingness to split the party over the race issue was a direct calculation and crucial to his presumed chances at winning the election.[23]

But people remained unhappy with the president. They continued to question both his judgment and his leadership. As Zachary Karabell notes, "As of March 1948, Harry Truman was being opposed from within his own party, from the left and from the right and from the center. He . . . appeared to be on the verge of political death. The Republicans could sense the victory that had eluded them since Herbert Hoover's win in 1928."[24] By April of 1948, Truman and the electorate had enough evidence that multiple forces were coalescing to unseat his election bid. His approval rating with the American people was a paltry 36 percent.[25] A new Gallup poll indicated that President Truman was trailing the top four potential Republican presidential candidates: Thomas E. Dewey, Harold E. Stassen, Arthur Vandenberg, and Douglas MacArthur.[26] *The*

New Republic's April 5th cover story summarized a growing sentiment: "Truman Should Quit." The magazine's editor, Michael Straight, asserted brusquely: "The president of the United States today is the leader of world democracy. Truman has neither the vision nor the strength that leadership demands."[27]

Such blatant public votes of no confidence were nuisances Truman learned to take with a grain of salt. While he was being peppered from various quarters with insults and protests regarding his weaknesses, he was not about to let the press and other politicians outrun his own predilections and instincts. Truman was a realist: he knew his confidence was seen as misplaced, both by his opponents and his friends since neither gave him much chance of winning the election. In 1964, Truman described his 1948 predicament rather cogently: "If the angels were on my side, they were about the only ones who were."[28]

The president had decided that an all-out campaign that was targeted directly to the people would be just the thing to wake up the country and not coincidently enliven his sagging popularity at the polls. He had concluded that no one else could carry the Democratic banner in quite the same way. Truman's loyalty to New Deal liberalism had particular importance for both foreign and domestic policy in the United States. Harry Truman wanted to continue in the tradition of FDR and make a few inroads himself. This could only be accomplished if he stayed on the watch and stayed the course. Truman recalled, "I made up my mind long before the convention that I was going to be a candidate because I knew if I backed out, it would look as if I had felt I hadn't done the job as I thought it should be done, and I thought that if I could get out in the country and see and talk to the people, we would win."[29]

The president's optimism, however, seemed a bit overblown, especially given his lackluster reputation as a public orator. Robert Ferrell describes the president as "a deplorable speaker."[30] Truman had trouble delivering a prepared text. As Robert Donovan notes, "The moment he started to read a speech his voice went flat. His delivery was monotonous."[31] Moreover, even if the speechwriters tried to liven up things a bit by adding a little light-hearted banter, the president "was so inept at reading aloud that he could never have read prepared humor in a way that would permit it to sound spontaneous."[32] In addition, as Donald R. McCoy has observed, "His voice was flat and nasal, his prepared texts were often stilted, and his gestures were limited to chopping hand motions, which were not always appropriate to what he was saying. He did not look the statesman, and he did not have the offsetting appeal of youth."[33] Such real and perceived deficits seemed formidable. They did not inspire confidence in Truman's ability to persuade and ultimately win over a restless electorate.

A New Rhetorical Approach

In April and May of 1948, Truman stumbled upon a new way to ensure that he would at least get a fair hearing. The president tested the rhetorical waters by speaking extemporaneously. His advisers were particularly interested in what the president's extemporaneous approach might sound like on the radio.

Truman's memory of the shift to an extemporaneous oratorical style is informative. It demonstrates the importance of developing a style that was less dependent on the written text, and it helps account for the origins of his whistle-stop remarks: "My first formal experience at extemporaneous speaking had come just a few weeks before I opened the whistle-stop tour in June. After reading an address to the American Society of Newspaper Editors in April, I decided to talk 'off-the-cuff' on American relations with Russia. When I finished my remarks about thirty minutes later, I was surprised to get the most enthusiastic applause that I had ever received from a group made up of mostly Republicans." In a live radio broadcast on May 6, Truman spoke for thirteen minutes before the National Conference on Family Life. In the extemporaneous mode, the president seemed comfortable, direct, and even affable. Some of the flatness in his voice dissipated. Aides were pleased with the performance. The president himself began to recognize the utility of the approach: "On May 14 I again tried my hand at speaking without a manuscript when I addressed a rally of the Young Democrats in Washington. A New York newspaper called the speech a 'fighting one in the new Truman manner.' I decided that if speaking without a prepared copy or getting away from reading a prepared text was more effective in getting my ideas across, I would use that method on the trainside talks that I planned to make in the future." Indeed, Truman was so pleased with the results that he exclaimed, "It was a style which I was to follow in my acceptance speech at the Democratic convention and in most of the speeches I was to deliver in the Campaign from Labor Day up to the November election."[34]

Truman clearly did not enjoy delivering a prepared text. As indicated earlier, the prepared text was often unfriendly in Truman's hands and his delivery and inflection suffered as a result. Truman's delivery was too fast and largely monotone. His Missouri twang struck some as alien. He lost eye contact with his audience as he read the manuscript in front of him and, at times, he lost his place. In delivering a prepared text, Truman seemed to have only one gesture, an awkward two-handed downward chopping motion. Extemporaneous address reduced these negative qualities and gave the president a more immediate presence with his audience. Ad-libbed remarks also allowed the president a certain comfort level, and his natural gift for banter provided a genuine warmth, which steered audiences away from any suspicion of a crafted public relations image. Another benefit was that the president was able to incorporate his own homespun humor—something the prepared texts simply did not afford. The "new Truman" emerged as a feisty, engaged speaker, brimming with ideas on policies and programs important to the common citizen. His arguments were delivered in a direct, no nonsense, unvarnished, people-friendly fashion. When the president extemporized, audiences felt he was telling them the truth and "pulled no punches." The newly minted forthright approach allowed Truman to "give 'em Hell!" It released him from the straight-laced formality of the prepared text and allowed him to develop a more natural, more comfortable, and perhaps an even more congruous and audience-friendly public *persona.* In short, Truman's extemporaneous stump speaking allowed him to become, in Alonzo Hamby's words, a "man of the people." The first great experiment employing Truman's newly reinvigorated rhetorical approach would emerge more concretely on his planned "nonpolitical" train trip west in June of 1948.

CHAPTER 2

The Western Tour, June 1948

Unlike today, when presidential campaigns commence more than a year before the election, Truman's official campaign was slated to begin on Labor Day. The president was restless, however, and determined that he needed a head start. In June of 1948, a *New York Times* editorial commented:

> President Truman ... is tired of reading that he cannot win. ... Polls show him around rock bottom. The South is still rumbling. Henry Wallace keeps sawing at the democratic limb. But Mr. Truman has a wide streak of Missouri in him, and the home-state dentist who suggested that it was time to back out of the race got his answer: 'I was not brought up to run from a fight.' So Mr. Truman decide[d] that it is time to be aggressive on a grand scale. The trip to the Pacific is the full challenge of a battle to all his foes, in or out of the Democratic Party. If he feels private doubts, this tour may resolve them. The national campaign, at any rate, is definitely on.[1]

While early on some Truman forces might have publicly dismissed the charge that the national campaign was now "definitely on," there was some private consensus on the matter. At a minimum, the advice from the Rowe-Clifford memorandum on the importance of the West to the president's chances of being elected certainly seemed to be taken seriously with the onset of this trip. Truman had received an invitation from the University of California, Berkeley, to deliver a commencement address in June of 1948. He used the invitation as an opportunity to tour the West by rail and deliver five major speeches at larger cities—including Chicago, Omaha, Seattle, Berkeley, and Los Angeles—as well as dozens of rear-platform remarks to smaller towns and cities along the route. Many of the rear-platform talks were scheduled for broadcast over the local radio stations. While the *Times* was correct about Truman's intentions and many felt that the trip had implications for the 1948 campaign, administration aides steadfastly labeled the trip "nonpolitical." Harry S. Truman seemed bemused by, and largely ignored, the label—and as the trip unfolded it was hard to identify this particular rail tour as anything but a sure-fire, high-octane pre-campaign test. GOP National Party Chair Carroll Reece certainly viewed the trip with a skeptical eye: "Let his friends call it 'non-political,'" he said, "but it will be as 'non-political' as the Pendergast machine."[2] Truman's western train tour would be his first transcontinental trip since assuming the presidency.

The rail tour began June 3, 1948, with a first stop in Crestline, Ohio, June 4. The train then made its way through Indiana with scheduled stops in Fort Wayne and Gary and proceeded on to Chicago where Truman made his first major speech. June 5 and 6 Truman traveled through Nebraska and Wyoming, June 7 and 8 he made stops in Idaho and Montana, June 9 and 10 he toured the state of Washington, and on June 11, he passed through Oregon, making numerous stops. The president made California a major stop June 12 through 14, traversed Arizona and New Mexico on June 15, made a number of stops in Kansas on June 16, and on June 17 made home-state stops in Missouri. On the return trip to Washington, Truman's train stopped again in Illinois, Indiana, and Ohio. By June 18 the train had passed through Pennsylvania and Maryland. It then returned to Washington, D.C.

Upon leaving Washington, D.C., to embark on his western tour, Truman was typically upbeat, telling reporters, "If I felt any better, I couldn't stand it." He would depart in a sixteen-car train, which contained the president's personal air-conditioned car, the *Ferdinand*

Magellan. The presidential train also was equipped with a car for the secretariat, a White House office staff car, a staff bedroom car, four press bedroom cars, a press work room and lounge, two dining cars, four cars for railroad workers, a car for White House staff overflow and transients, and a signal car at the rear. Traveling with the president were his wife, Bess, and daughter, Margaret; presidential appointments secretary Matthew Connelly; press secretary Charles G. Ross; Special Counsel Clark Clifford; Charles S. Murphy, who served as an administrative assistant and speechwriter; Gen. Wallace A. Graham, White House physician; a number of military aides; and James M. Maloney, chief of the Secret Service. The president's personal secretary, Miss Rose Conway, and the reputedly lightning-fast stenographer, Jack Romagna, were also on board to help out. In addition to the president's immediate party and White House staff members, there were some sixty members of the press, including newspaper reporters, radio broadcasters, and photographers. The entourage also included a full complement of railroad guards and maintenance and service personnel. Each of the participants would gain valuable experience for the campaign ahead.[3] A few highlights from the June western rail trip revealed the flavor of the developing campaign atmosphere, the tenor of the president's remarks and the crowd response, and how this particular trip provided a learning curve for Truman and his staff as they looked ahead to the fall campaign.

The western trip of June 3–18 was a successive sea of back-platform speeches, major addresses, motorcades, flags, bunting, marching bands, drum majors and majorettes, cowboys on horseback, and cheering parade stands. The trip had all the markings of a political campaign. Truman was aware of the criticism he was receiving for his so-called "nonpolitical" tour. At Crestline, Ohio, he joked, "This is a nonpartisan and bipartisan trip, but I understand there are some Democrats along too!"[4] The line received a laugh. At an early stop in Gary, Indiana, "surrounded by factories and filled with a large crowd of workers," Truman railed against the Eightieth Congress, telling the assemblage that Congress was more concerned with interest groups like the National Association of Manufacturers and the National Chamber of

Commerce than about high prices and the need for price controls. He asked those assembled to work on delivering a new Congress—one that had a record defending the interests of "the common people" rather than "the interests of the men who have all the money."[5]

Truman's first major address was June 4, 1948, in Chicago. Addressing the Swedish Pioneer Centennial Association, the president immediately struck a populist theme, "When I think of the great epics in our history, like the Swedish immigration of a century ago, I am reminded again of the source of our strength as a nation. Early settlers in the United States came here to escape harsh restrictions on personal liberties in their homelands, or to find economic opportunity. Here the people were proud to be democratic, and they looked on individual liberty as something sacred. The law recognized no aristocracy, and a man was respected according to his own merits. The rights of the little man were just as important as the rights of the big man. And we must fight today to see that America stays that way." Truman also shared his thoughts on communism, which stood in stark contrast to his depiction of U.S.-style democracy: "Communism exalts the state and degrades the individual; communism holds that the individual is only a means to an end; communism holds that the duty of the individual is to conform to the state's definition of what is good for him. This we are against. We must resist it, and we must provide aid and hope to those in the world who resist it. But we cannot resist it with our full strength unless we all work for the success of our democracy continually and reaffirm our faith in that democracy."[6] In arguing that U.S. ideals, premised on shared beliefs in democracy, freedom, and equality, were the best defense against communism and that those same ideals could provide "hope for those who resist it," Truman was defending his world view against those who interpreted Soviet international relations a bit differently and opposed the measures Truman had already taken to realize his vision.

But Truman's appearances were not only helping the nation focus on issues such as the rights of the common citizen and the need for principled vigilance to control communist expansion, they were also opportunities for transmitting the president's newly minted image.

The people seemed to react positively to the man they were seeing for themselves for the first time. As one internal summary noted, "At all the stops men and women were heard to remark on Mr. Truman's appearance. Apparently the close-up they were getting did not seem to fit their preconceptions. 'He's not a bad-looking guy, is he?' said a man on Jackson Boulevard in Chicago."[7]

At a parade in Omaha, an incontestably Republican-dominated city, the president shared a car with the mayor and the governor of Oklahoma. Mindful of his need to appeal to veterans, Truman paused to wait for his old military unit, Battery D of the 129th Field Artillery, to join him in the parade so they could march along. After about a block of marching, the ex-soldiers in his old unit started to "taunt him good-naturedly." "What's the matter with old Harry—why can't he walk with us?" they teased. "Why the hell can't Harry walk?" Truman, donning a "gabardine suit" with "a red Battery D brassard on his right arm," had been waiting for the signal to get out of the car and march with his comrades. Having decided he had waited long enough, he jumped down to meet his smiling cohort and walked with them for about a half mile until he came to the presidential reviewing stand where he took in the rest of the parade. As testimony at the time suggested, "The crowd enjoyed seeing the President marching and gave him an even heartier reception than the Chicagoans who saw him yesterday."[8] The president was enjoying himself as much as the crowd enjoyed seeing him. More importantly, Truman demonstrated a knack for embodying the common man he championed. His actions were consistent with his rhetoric. Who but Harry Truman would jump out of his automobile on a parade route and march good-naturedly with his old war buddies?

In Omaha later that day things did not go so swimmingly. The June 21 issue of *Life* magazine highlighted a public relations fiasco—a photograph of rows and rows of empty seats at a Truman rally at Omaha's Aksar-Ben auditorium. A caption accompanying the photo was doubly embarrassing: it informed readers that the president had spoken to "a nearly empty auditorium in Omaha." The president also received negative coverage of the event from major newspapers such as the *New York Times,* the *St. Louis Post-Dispatch,* and the *Washington*

Times-Herald, the latter of which labeled the rally a real "floperoo."[9] Public relations disasters in Omaha and elsewhere provided needed lessons in planning and logistics for the upcoming fall campaign.

Despite the occasional well-known glitches, the western trip also seemed to be working it own magic. Truman was making a mark for himself. As reporter Niel Johnson wrote, "Very few would say that he had flamboyance or charisma. Most would say he has extraordinary integrity. Whatever else he had, he showed an ability to relate to many people at all levels." The president's popularity was attributed to his "directness and plainness of speech." Truman's "simple, modest friendliness in back platform appearances" were reportedly receiving "a good-natured response from these crowds regardless of party affiliations." Mr. Truman was garnering a reputation as "one of our least pretentious Presidents." He "displayed an unusual ability to balance the dignity of his office with a willingness to meet people honestly and directly at whatever level he found them." Truman conveyed an easy "self-confidence without conceit."[10] He started to build his political and rhetorical ethos. Audiences were beginning to realize that perhaps having a man in the Oval Office without pretensions—one who spoke in a clear, direct, straightforward, and friendly manner—was not such a liability after all.

The president seemed to rally from the small turnout in Omaha. He received an enthusiastic reception on Sunday June 6 "as his train moved slowly across Nebraska and Wyoming." When he stopped at Grand Island, Nebraska, some four thousand people waited to greet him. The unscripted moments and remarks made for some festive and feisty encounters. Added color was provided by rodeo queen Miss Ruth Kuester and Ed White Buffalo, a Sioux Indian. Miss Kuester handed Mr. Truman a pair of "gleaming spurs," and a man in the crowd shouted, "Put 'em on, Harry!" The president smiled and retorted, "When I get them, I can take the Congress to town. I'll give them a trial just as soon as I get back to Washington." Ed White Buffalo, in full-feathered traditional dress, sidled up to the train with his two-year-old son and proudly presented Mr. Truman with a peace pipe. At the same stopover, a little girl handed Bess Truman a beautiful bouquet of orchids.

When he arrived in Idaho, Truman was greeted by a group of children who regaled him with gifts that included chewing gum and jelly beans. Truman started paying more attention to the children whose smiling faces were always there to greet him. Their cherubic presence gave an added sense of the impact of his persona as the nation's leader and role model; he basked warmly in the heartfelt admiration that the young folk always provided.[11] At Pocatello, defending himself against the long shadow of suspicion cast his way by his association with the Pendergast machine that had helped launch his earlier political career, the president averred in typical colloquial style, but nonetheless emphatically, "I have been in politics a long time, and it makes no difference what they say about you, if it isn't so. If they can prove it on you, you are in a bad fix indeed. They never have been able to prove it on me."[12]

Not all were happy with the president's excursion. Some party leaders in Nebraska, Iowa, and Montana felt they had received "the bum's rush" in the planning for the visits, and some even threatened to withdraw their support from Truman at the upcoming nominating convention. At Carey, Idaho, there was a bit of an embarrassing mix-up. Truman had spoken to Mr. and Mrs. Sheldon Coates whose son, he had been informed, had died in the war, and whose name subsequently was attached to the local airport. It turned out that the Coates' daughter was actually the one who had died, and she, Wilma Coates, was the person whose name was attached to the airport. Incidents like these left a few fences to mend. They were the kind of thing Truman hoped to avoid through more careful preparation and planning in the fall. Despite these rough spots, Truman basked in the hurly-burly of the campaign-like atmosphere. It suited his temperament and increased his confidence about the road ahead.

At Spokane, and again at the Grand Coulee Dam, where the president participated in the dedication of a new power generator, Truman gave voters a preview of the upcoming fall campaign, charging that the Eightieth Congress was the "worst" in history; he qualified his statement slightly by mentioning that an earlier Congress, which had reached ignominy with Thaddeus Stevens—the Radical Republican who led the charge to impeach Andrew Johnson during the early Reconstruction era—might have been worse, but the press was more concerned with his opinion on the Eightieth, and Truman told them that they could let his charge stand.

The Republicans found this "worst Congress" talk distasteful, to say the least, and they fired back. House majority leader Charles A. Halleck of Indiana allowed that the charge was a bit odd since some people felt that Harry Truman was "the poorest President we have had since George Washington was elected," and furthermore, there was "no doubt that this Congress has had the worst cooperation from the White House that any Congress has had." Sen. Kenneth E. Wherry of Nebraska, indignant at Truman's blatant partisanship, remarked icily, "That's a curious statement from the non-political, bi-partisan investigation that the President said he was making."[13]

While the political nature of the trip was by now largely indisputable, at Bremerton some thought that Truman's increasingly populist discourse had crossed the line by invoking class warfare: "You know, this Congress is interested in the welfare of the better classes. They are not interested in the welfare of the common, everyday man." While the president continued to press this point, some in the crowds would egg him on, shouting, "Pour it on, Harry!" And the president shot back, "I'm going to, I'm going to." And pour it on he did. With gusto.[14]

While Truman poured it on, the GOP decided it could not remain silent. On June 11, 1948, potential presidential candidate Sen. Robert A. Taft countered Truman's attack on the Eightieth Congress with his now-famous complaint that the president was "blackguarding Congress at every whistle station in the West." The Democratic National Committee seized upon a political opportunity in the remarks and telegraphed a number of the hamlets, towns, and cities scheduled for Truman's visits to inquire whether the inhabitants considered their town or city a mere "whistle-stop." The overwhelming response was one of indignation.[15]

As one newspaper account noted, "Whistle-Stop? That's a tank town, a hamlet, a mere place in the road. The Democrats actually had wired 35 places across the country where Mr. Truman had spoken on his 'nonpolitical' rail tour. They posed the question: Was it nice of the senator to call you a whistle-stop? (Taft didn't mention any particular communities.)." Predictably, these small communities were quick to express their displeasure. Laramie, Wyoming, replied that Senator Taft was "confused." Gary, Indiana, felt Taft's remarks were "in very poor taste." Crestline, Ohio, suggested that Mr. Taft consult the "timetables" to determine how many passenger trains stop there regularly. And Mayor Fletcher Brown of Los Angeles quipped, "Anyone who could have been in Los Angeles last Monday . . . and witnessed nearly 1,000,000 good American citizens lining the streets to welcome their President, would have both whistled and stopped."[16] The indignation may have been manufactured and fanned by the Democrats, but locals were not amused at the slight.

In Eugene, Oregon, in a back-platform remark he would later regret, Truman caused quite a diplomatic stir when he blurted, "I like old Joe Stalin. He is a good fellow, but he is a prisoner of the Politburo."[17] The remark was not in keeping with Truman's emerging reputation as a cold warrior and a staunch anticommunist. When Clifford and Ross approached the president and tactfully but forcefully informed him that he had committed a verbal diplomatic blunder, the president responded, "Well I guess I goofed."[18]

Interestingly, the gaffes made on the western trip, including ill-considered remarks, became such a source of concern that the president's advisers began to rethink and retool their strategy. As George M. Elsey notes, "Clifford, Murphy, and I were of one mind. The Democratic National Committee must quickly assemble a cluster of bright, energetic, and imaginative young men (in 1948, one didn't think of 'young women') to research every city and every situation in which Truman would appear during the actual campaign scheduled to begin on Labor Day."[19] This was accomplished when the Democratic National Committee appointed William "Bill" Batt to head a research support group that directly assisted the speechwriting team crucial to Truman's later success in the fall.

Just as the miscues on the train tour were instructive, so too were Truman's remarks on the back platform at the various train stops.

His stop in Everett, Washington, on June 9, 1948, was representative. In Everett, we encounter a typical early example of how the president was slowly developing a comfortable and effective pattern for his back-platform speeches.

First, acknowledge state and local officials present and acknowledge the turnout. Truman appeared with Gov. Mon C. Wallgren, Sen. Warren Magnuson, Everett mayor Henry Arends, and Frank A. Banks, district manager of the Grand Coulee Dam.

> Thank you, Mon. I am not fooled a bit. This crowd turned out for the home town boy who is Governor of Washington. And that is just exactly what they should have done.
>
> Mr. Mayor, I can't tell you how very much I appreciated that cordial welcome. I am overwhelmed at the turnout, even though Mon is on the train. I have been here before on two different occasions. I came here and spent the time with Mon Wallgren at his home, when his father and mother were living here. And I don't know when I have ever met a person I thought more of than I did of Mon's father. His mother is a grand person—she is just like my mother—she raised a good son, and here he is.
>
> You know, a boy or a girl reflects his parents, and I think Mon is a shining example of a good beginning.

Second, demonstrate a personal connection with the local area and a familiarity with local issues.

> I have been in this State all day—started at Spokane—got in a car—went up to the Grand Coulee Dam. I have been there twice before, but I have never seen as much water in my life. And I have seen the Missouri and the Mississippi in flood stage, and I have been to Niagara, and I have been up the Hudson. I have not seen the Yukon, but I have seen every other river in the United States.
>
> The Columbia is really on a rampage, and I am sorry. They tell me there has never been a flood like it since 1894. Well, in 1903 we

had a flood on the Missouri River, and they said there never had been another like it since 1844. That's a long time, too. My grandmother saw both floods, and she said the 1903 one was worse than the 1844 flood. There were no houses or buildings there, and that was true here in 1894—there wasn't anything on the Columbia River to wash away so nobody heard about it.

I came out here at the suggestion of your Governor to see what could be done to complete the development of the Columbia River from a power, reclamation, irrigation, and flood control standpoint.

Third, compliment the region, especially making clear those contributions that can be connected to the national interest. If possible, add a personal touch or anecdote to reinforce identification with the audience. When appropriate, add a little humor into the mix.

I brought a lot of reporters with me on this trip, and I venture to say there isn't half of them ever saw anything west of the Appalachian Mountains. Now they are going to find out where the country lies! And where the resources of the country come from. And I hope they will tell their eastern readers and constituents just exactly what they have seen in the last 3 or 4 days. If they do, we will have a united country for the development of our resources, and the things that make us great.

You know, this Northwest section made one of the greatest contributions to the war that was made in the whole setup. We would have had a hard time winning the war if it hadn't been for this Northwest power section.

I had an old man testifying before a committee of which I was chairman, and Senator Wallgren at that time was a member of that committee, and that old man in a high, squeaky voice told us that the Aluminum Company of America was making 300 million pounds of aluminum. At that time that was all the country needed. Well, you know what we are making now—3500 million pounds now, and we are short! If it hadn't been for these power plants, we never could have made aluminum and magnesium and the things that are necessary to win the war.

The reference to the contributions made by the region to the war effort also afforded Truman the opportunity to speak about his own military service in World War I while simultaneously having a little fun at the governor's expense. The interaction highlighted Truman's credibility and his humility:

> Truman: I was a captain of field artillery in the other war. Wallgren here was a lieutenant of field artillery. I outranked him.
> Governor Wallgren: As he does now.
> Truman: Mon, I wasn't going to say that. Because in the great State of Washington—and I am talking protocol to you now—the Governor is the ranking officer in the State. The President is only his guest. Don't let anybody fool you on that.

Truman could not resist a political appeal before concluding his back-platform remarks: "In 1920 we should have assumed the leadership which Almighty God intended us to assume. We have got another chance now. We are rated as the greatest and most powerful nation in the world. We want to use that greatness and that power for the welfare of the world, just as we have used it for the welfare of the forty-eight states of the Union. And that can be done, and we must do it!"

Fourth, thank all present for their support and their attendance. "I can't tell you how very much I appreciate this cordial welcome in the hometown of the Governor of Washington, my friend Senator Wallgren, which his title was then, on the so-called Truman committee when I was in the Senate. Thank you very much."

After his remarks, a number of people sidled up to the train to shower the president with gifts. After being presented with a fishing rod and reel, the president remarked humorously, "I am more than happy to receive this rod and reel on this bipartisan, nonpolitical trip of mine. Over at Sun Valley, I had a lot of lessons in casting, with a rod not half as good or half as light as this one. And I will tell you what I am going to do. When things warm up, and we get into politics, I am going to take this rod out and try to catch votes as well as fish with it." Someone else presented him with a shirt: "Well, it's all right! I will accept it, and I will wear it. It's well made—seems to be out of a good piece of cloth. I will have to examine it with a microscope to be sure [laughter]—but I know that the citizens of Everett wouldn't give me anything that wasn't all right." Another person handed the president a local salmon derby entry form:

> Thank you very much for that. As you remember, when I was out here the last time, Mon and I went fishing, and Mon had a sweater made by the Siwash Indians. When they saw that sweater on me, they made me one. It is much better looking than Mon's. Look what I have here now, from my Fraternal Members of the Order of Eagles! Isn't that something!
>
> Well, I will make use of it. I don't think I will have any chance to use it in the salmon derby, because I don't know what the conditions are, but I want to say to you I am going to do that just like I do everything else, I am going to do my damndest![20]

This kind of folksy banter placed the president in a favorable light. Audiences were warming to the president's easy manner and homespun chit-chat. While there is some truth to the claim that "the farther west Truman traveled the taller the corn grew—in field and in rhetoric," it did not seem to detract from the president's reception.[21] These kinds of exchanges were fast becoming an endearing ingredient that people assembled at the next stop seemed to anticipate with relish.

Wherever the president stopped, upon concluding his remarks, he would peer out at the audience and ask, "How'd ya' like to meet my wife and daughter?" This always provoked cheers and applause, and Mr. Truman, obliging the crowd, said, "Well, I'll present Mrs. Truman first." Truman often teased the audience, "You really want to meet my family, do ya? Alright, I'll call the boss out first!" Bess would come out from behind a royal blue curtain smiling and waving. After bringing Bess out on the back platform, he would smile and say, "Now here's Margaret!" These appearances by Bess and Margaret, while scripted, were quite popular; they were not only welcomed but became one of the expected highlights of the president's train stops. Bess and Margaret were often presented with bouquets of flowers or other mementos at each appearance. These gifts were added to those received by the president; those tokens of appreciation were soon taking up a lot of space on the train. When there was time, before leaving for the next stop the president would often bend over the railing on the back platform to shake hands and greet well-wishers.[22]

The major speeches on the trip west took on a particularly political tone. For example, on Saturday, June 12, at 3:55 PM EDT, Harry S. Truman stood before a throng estimated at well over fifty thousand people to deliver a commencement address at the University of California, Berkeley. This gathering had attracted twice as many people as any prior commencement address at the Berkeley campus. Berkeley's president, Dr. Robert Gordon Sproul, awarded Truman the traditional honorary doctoral degree.

The president told the assembled throng that his purpose was to "appraise the progress we are making toward world peace." He maintained that "Anyone can talk peace. But only the work that is done for peace really counts." After reviewing a number of initiatives the United States had undertaken to advance the peace process, including fighting in World War II, working to establish and implement the United Nations and related agencies, proposing international control of atomic energy, and contributing nearly twenty billion dollars in loans and grants to other nations, Truman proclaimed, "This is a record of action in behalf of peace without parallel in history." He lamented the Soviet Union's lack of cooperation in the international arena: "The refusal of the Soviet Union to work with its wartime allies for world recovery and world peace is the most bitter disappointment of our time." Truman denied that his critique was based solely on conflict between the United States and the Soviet Union: "We are not engaged in a struggle with the Soviet Union for any territory or for any economic gain. We have no hostile or aggressive designs against the Soviet Union or any other country. We are not waging a 'cold war.' The cleavage that exists is not between the Soviet Union and the United States. It is between the Soviet Union and the rest of the world. The great questions at stake today affect not only the United States and the Soviet Union; they affect all nations." In this way, Truman tried to redefine the issue as something different from bilateral competition and mere bellicosity. He asked the Soviets to honor world standards already in place.

While the United States remained "strongly devoted to the principle of discussion and negotiation," certain activities were non-negotiable: "There is nothing to negotiate when one nation disregards the principles of international conduct to which all the members of the United Nations have subscribed. There is nothing to negotiate when one nation habitually uses coercion and open aggression in international affairs. What the world needs in order to regain a sense of security is an end to Soviet obstruction and aggression." Only then, said the president, can the paths to peace be realized: "What is needed is a will for peace. What is needed is the abandonment of the absurd idea that the capitalistic nations will collapse and that the instability in international affairs will hasten their collapse, leaving the world free for communism. It is possible for different economic systems to live side by side in peace, one with the other, provided one of these systems is not determined to destroy the other by force."

Truman's defense of U.S. policy was also buttressed by American principles: "The only prize we covet is the respect and good will of our fellow members of the family of nations. The only realm in which we aspire to eminence exists in the minds of men, where authority is exercised through the qualities of sincerity, compassion and right conduct. Abiding devotion to these ideals, and profound faith in their ultimate triumph, sustain and guide the American people in the service of the most compelling cause of our time—the crusade for peace."[23] In setting these clear parameters, Truman was engaging in some early campaigning. In issuing assurances that his leadership was principled and that his intentions were focused on peace, he was addressing the fears of war directly. He was also trying to blunt the force of Henry A. Wallace and his Progressive Party's challenge to his brand of international diplomacy. Wallace had announced his third-party candidacy just over six months earlier. Wallace believed Truman was building an emerging "military-industrial complex," and Wallace wanted none of it. For Truman, initiatives like the Marshall Plan were crucial to thwarting the communist threat and preserving the peace. The president felt that the world needed an end to Soviet expansionism and that the United States's mission in the post–World War II era was to "keep strong for the sake of peace."

Aides who had traveled with the president on the train detected that the boss had gained a few more friends, but their feelings could not be reliably confirmed. One thing was certain: the trip west had taken its toll in exhaustion. By the time the president got to Ash Fork, Arizona, on Tuesday, June 16, he exclaimed, "I have never been so tired in all my life."[24] The western trip allowed Truman to hone his rhetorical skills and to test what worked with his audiences and what did not. Major speeches and back-platform remarks on the president's daunting speaking tour actually provided a rhetorical laboratory of immeasurable benefit.

Significant Lessons

The western trip provided significant lessons that the president could later use to his advantage. The tour had given Truman a chance to test a newfound mode of populism. Just as important, the stops on the tour were opportunities to raise funds for the party and the campaign that was to follow. In addition, the president learned that, for all its faults, his traveling road show placed him in a prime position with his constituents. Even the planning miscues and rhetorical blunders seemed to be assisting the president in his efforts to create publicity for himself. "Unmistakably, the blend of error, comedy, folksiness, and political head-splitting was stirring great curiosity about Truman's itinerant Punch-and-Judy show, and the crowds grew larger as it moved along."[25] The president seemed to have an uncanny ability to take any adversity that presented itself and turn it to his advantage.

When the trip ended, press accounts noted a "new" Truman: "folksy, hearty, and humorous." They spoke of his fighting stance and his growing ability to meet his attackers head on. There was an old-fashioned "frontier" quality to Truman's political musings on the hustings, and his railing against a "do-nothing" Congress and the rich had an edge and an energy that demonstrated he might still be someone to reckon with. The president even lectured his audiences about responsible voting. Nonetheless, no one in the press corps was willing to concede that his chances of being elected had gained any substantial ground. Still, "the campaign had benefited from a trial run."[26]

According to Elsey, the June western trip was useful for at least two reasons. First, "the President discovered . . . that his policy of trying to get Congress to enact his program had not been getting through to the American people." Second, he began to realize the "the sins of the 80th Congress were being blamed on him." Problems like scarce housing, high prices, flood control, and rural electrification all seemed to be heaped upon his shoulders. That is when he determined to "give a new kind of speech and he took a new approach. He began a series of open, blunt attacks on Congress, calling it the worst in American history. Item by item, in seventy speeches he reviewed the requests he had made of Congress and Congress's action on them. He dramatized the clash between the President and Congress and between the Democrats and Republicans." As importantly, the June trip had "laid the pattern that the president was to follow in the coming campaign," and "greatly increased his popularity, assuring his nomination at Philadelphia. Before his western tour nobody would have given a plug nickel for his chances of being nominated, but after the trip he had little trouble."[27]

The western tour also served as a trial run for attending to the indispensable nuts and bolts that held together any successful campaign by rail. Undersecretary of the Interior Oscar L. Chapman, a native Coloradoan, was charged with making prior arrangements for the train tour. His job was to precede the president, organize the itinerary, and smooth the way for the stops ahead. As Chapman testifies, "I was advance man on all the President's trips, contacting the politicians . . . and labor leaders, and making all detailed arrangements for his

[Truman's] appearances, even down to the people who were to be introduced to him. In fact, I had everything to do but wash the dishes at the buffet supper we gave him in Los Angeles."[28] Chapman's role on the western train tour proved invaluable for future campaign trips in the fall. As Clifford notes, "We needed advance men at every stop at least a day ahead of the President; this was a technique that was to become a routine part of all campaigning but was used then only for major occasions."[29]

Not only did the staff hone its skills in developing itineraries, making proper arrangements, and ensuring that key dignitaries were in place and satisfied, but Truman discovered that speaking from an outline, from which he could depart at will, served him much better than a prepared speech text, which he found hard to read and often delivered in lackluster fashion. Employing this new approach in his public address lifted his speeches off the page and out to the audiences who appreciated the feisty, straightforward discourse to which they were being treated. Truman had found a speaking format that more suited his style and temperament, and it even gave him some pleasure, a rare commodity associated with his past faltering rhetorical efforts. The president's new approach quickened his spirits, freed his thoughts, and enlivened his enthusiasm as the crowds began to respond favorably to his words. One scholar has argued that the president's "new" rhetorical effectiveness was redolent of the thirty-seven-year-old Truman's political barnstorming in his election campaign for eastern county judge of Jackson County in Missouri.[30]

The president's reinvigorated speaking style was like finding an old friend again and striking up the most intensely gratifying conversation. The rhythm, tone, and arrangement all seemed to fit like a glove. Aides were enthusiastic. "The Boss" seemed at home and wholly comfortable with his newly recovered speaking persona. Truman's newfound style of stump speaking even started to influence his attempts in more formal settings.[31] Chapman's overall assessment of the June trip was quite positive: "All's well that ends well and I think that the President's trip to the West ended up in an atmosphere of success that surprised a great many people."[32] It allowed Truman to highlight important issues, address the crowds in a friendly and direct manner, and add a little humor into the folksy mix. The only thing missing was an invitation to vote for him in November. The president seemed to use the western trip to find his stride. Perhaps most importantly, the tour helped establish a theme, fine-tune a rhythm, and set a tone that suited the president and would prove useful in the drive for votes in the fall. First, however, he would have to get his party's nomination for the presidency.

The Democratic National Convention and the Special Session of Congress, July 1948

On Monday, July 12, the Democrats took their turn at holding a nominating convention in Philadelphia. It was a somber, almost gruesome midsummer event. Despite the challenges on the left from Wallace's Progressive Party and the rumblings of disaffection over the president's civil rights program in the South, Truman's nomination was now viewed as a foregone conclusion. One week prior to the convention northern liberals and southern segregationists led by Claude Pepper mounted an effort to draft Gen. Dwight Eisenhower, but Ike refused and Truman was the only candidate with enough support to be nominated. Given the president's poll numbers and the predictions of handicappers at the time, this knowledge did not create a lot of enthusiasm. Part of the doom-and-gloom atmosphere, then, came from the fact that it was largely believed—and voluminously reported—that Truman would lose the upcoming general election.

Sen. Alben Barkley, a revered icon of past New Deal–era conventions, delivered a rousing sixty-eight-minute keynote address that attacked the Republican-dominated Eightieth Congress for inaction, if not malfeasance. His old-fashioned, tent-pole-shaking oratory was met by

delegates with a spontaneous twenty-eight-minute celebration. After
being turned down by his first choice, Supreme Court Justice William
O. Douglas, Truman chose Barkley to fill the vice presidential slot on
the ticket. In Barkley, Truman had found an energetic and committed
seventy-year-old campaign warrior.[1]

One of the most contentious issues at the convention—and one that
was of utmost importance to the president—was the civil rights plank.
By the time the convention arrived, Truman found himself straddling
the fence on the civil rights issue. If the party platform went too far in
its endorsement of civil rights legislation, the states' rights proponents
in the South threatened to abandon the party. At a minimum, the
president risked the wrath of powerful southern politicians on crucial
committees, politicos whose decisions and directives could not only
wreak havoc on this domestic policy agenda but also potentially subvert
or block foreign policy initiatives where unity was paramount.[2]

A number of people were lining up to take aim at the party platform on civil rights. The president's aides sought a moderate plank
designed to soothe southern sensibilities and maintain party unity;
representatives from the South wanted to emphasize states' rights; and
more liberal members of the party wanted a more nuanced platform
endorsing specific policy proposals that had been enumerated in the
president's February 2 message. The maverick members of the "Draft
Eisenhower" group pledged that they would pursue the president's civil
rights initiatives: "The report of the President's Committee on Civil
Rights is one of the most important measures of moral strategy devised
by the United States of America in modern times.... We hereby declare
that we shall actively seek, at Philadelphia, to make the accomplishment
of this program a part of our party's platform for 1948."[3]

On July 14, 1948, the various groups clashed, and a number of different versions of the civil rights plank were introduced for consideration. A majority had approved the president's version, but some
liberals saw the wording as nothing more than abstract equivocation.
Hubert Humphrey, seeking endorsement of specific measures such
as anti-lynching laws, elimination of poll taxes, and establishment of
the Fair Employment Practices Commission, among others, speaking

for the more liberal wing of the party and in direct opposition to the president on this issue, thundered: "My friends, to those who say we are rushing this issue of civil rights, I say to them we are 172 years late. To those who say that this civil rights program is an infringement on states rights, I say this, that the time has arrived in America for the Democratic Party to get out of the shadows of states rights and to walk forthrightly into the bright sunshine of human rights."[4] Humphrey's speech would garner him national attention.

Meanwhile, southern opposition to civil rights produced three different opposing planks, one of which actually received a roll call vote but was ultimately defeated. To the president's presumed ultimate dismay, the plank Humphrey had defended, introduced by Andrew J. Biemiller of Wisconsin, was adopted. This plank later proved largely responsible for the subsequent Dixiecrat revolt. Indeed, southern Democrats' displeasure erupted instantaneously. As Berman notes, "Truman's efforts to preserve harmony came to naught, for immediately after the final civil rights vote was taken, half of the Alabama delegation, including Eugene Connor of Birmingham, followed by the entire Mississippi delegation, walked out of the convention."[5] Most southerners in Philadelphia chose to stay and cast their votes, but they directed them to a favorite son. Neither the walkout nor the protest vote would prevent the anticipated outcome. In the first round of balloting at the convention, Truman was nominated for president by a vote of 947 ½ to 263 for Sen. Richard Russell of Georgia.[6] While the outcome was favorable, as one pundit noted at the time, "Not in decades, if ever, has a major-party Presidential nomination been given more reluctantly than to President Truman."[7]

Distraught southern Democrats made their promised revolt official when delegates met on July 17 in Birmingham, Alabama, and nominated South Carolina governor Strom Thurmond for president and Mississippi governor Fielding L. Wright for vice president. These "states rights" Democrats hoped to generate enough support to block Truman from winning the general election.[8]

Democratic Platform

The themes for the upcoming campaign, first publicly articulated in the State of the Union Address and rehearsed with audiences during the June train tour, were set down in the final Democratic Platform of 1948. Predictably, the platform launched a scathing attack on the Republicans and set out a progressive, if not daunting, agenda. In the all-important domestic policy arena, it was noted, "The Republican 80th Congress is directly responsible for the existing and ever increasing high cost of living. It cannot dodge that responsibility." The Democrats promised to "curb the Republican inflation." They also blamed the housing shortage on the Republicans: "This nation is shamed by the failure of the Republican 80th Congress to pass vitally needed general housing legislation as recommended by the President. Adequate housing will end the need for rent control. Until then, it must be continued." And the Democrats complained that "the form of tax reduction adopted by the 80th Congress" had given "relief to those who need it least and ignored those who need it most." The platform courted labor in calling for "the repeal of the Taft-Hartley Act," which "was enacted by the Republican 80th Congress over the President's veto." It also advocated an extension of the Fair Labor Standards Act, a national health care program, federal aid to education, farm prosperity, federal relief services, and acknowledged the strengthened civil rights plank by commending the president "for his courageous stand on the issue of civil rights." The highly progressive platform also recommended a constitutional amendment on equal rights for women and called for the right of suffrage for the District of Columbia.[9] The platform was in sympathy with Truman's predispositions and played well to his strengths. It was fully supportable and gave the president even more ammunition to use against his Republican opponents. The next golden opportunity to engage his opponents, of course, came with the nomination acceptance address.

Nomination Acceptance Address

Batt sent Clifford a memo with a number of recommendations for the upcoming nomination address. The research director counseled that the president should deliver "a fighting talk" that would "keynote the entire campaign." Moreover, the effort "should not just exude confidence, but confidence with reasons." He urged delivery of a "short" speech employing "short phrases." Batt also attached an outline for Clifford, which highlighted the key issues he felt the president should address, including high prices, housing, education, and health care, among others.[10]

At approximately two o'clock in the morning, Harry Truman emerged from a stuffy dressing room and approached the podium in the full knowledge that he had been, as one newsreel announcer at the time had put it, "the last man in the world his party wanted to nominate for president."[11] Nevertheless, wearing a crisp white linen suit complemented by a dark tie and a neatly folded handkerchief in his vest pocket, the bespectacled nominee stepped to the podium with alacrity. The microphones were in place for a simultaneous national radio broadcast. Early on, the president set a populist tone: "The people know that the Democratic Party is the people's party, and the Republican Party is the party of special interest, and it always has been and always will be." Truman argued that the only source of "confidence and security" for the people would be found in solid support for the Democratic Party.

To prove his point, Truman depicted unparalleled prosperity for farmers and laborers under successive New Deal Democratic administrations, and he duly chided these particular constituents about the need for loyalty. Farmers and laborers were given an ultimatum in an argument that basically posed support for the president and his party as a moral obligation:

Farm income has increased from less than $2¼ billion in 1932 to more than $18 billion in 1947. Never in the world were the farmers of any republic or any kingdom or any other country as prosperous as the farmers of the United States; and if they don't do their duty by the Democratic Party, they are the most ungrateful people in the world!

Wages and salaries in this country have increased from $29 billion in 1933 to more than $128 billion in 1947. That's labor, and labor never had but one friend in politics, and that is the Democratic Party and Franklin D. Roosevelt.

And I say to labor what I have said to the farmers: they are the most ungrateful people in the world if they pass the Democratic Party by this year.

To the surprise of many inside and outside of the convention hall that morning, President Truman's delivery was quite lively. His voice alternated between enthusiastic exhortation and bristling anger. At times he would chop his right hand down while making a point; at others, he would emphasize his words with a downward two-hand chop. On different occasions, the president would raise both arms high up into the air, alternating all these gestures as he proceeded. The longer he spoke, the more animated both the voice and the gestures seemed to become.

Truman pounded the Eightieth Congress on issue after issue:

In the field of labor we needed moderate legislation to promote labor-management harmony, but Congress passed instead that so-called Taft-Hartley Act, which has disrupted labor-management relations and will cause strife and bitterness for years to come if it is not repealed, as the Democratic platform says it ought to be repealed.

I recommended an increase in the minimum wage. What did I get? Nothing. Absolutely nothing.

I have repeatedly asked the Congress to pass a health program. The Nation suffers from lack of medical care. That situation can be remedied any time the Congress wants to act upon it.

Everybody knows that I recommended to the Congress the civil rights program. I did that because I believed it to be my duty under the Constitution. Some of the members of my own party disagree with me violently on this matter. But they stand up and do it openly! People can tell where they stand. But the Republicans all professed to be for these measures. But Congress failed to act.

Truman also attacked the Republican Party platform as, at best, insincere: "They promised to do in that platform a lot of things I have been asking them to do that they have refused to do when they had the power." Having tarnished his opponents with charges of inaction and hypocrisy, Truman tried to rally the troops with a clarion call; this time the issue was social security: "The Republican platform is for extending and increasing social security benefits. Think of that! Increasing social security benefits! Yet when they had the opportunity, they took 750,000 off the social security rolls! I wonder if they think they can fool the people of the United States with such poppycock as that!" After relentlessly pummeling his Republican opponents on issue after issue, the president drew upon his ultimate trump card: "My duty as President requires that I use every means within my power to get the laws the people need on matters of such importance and urgency. I am therefore calling this Congress back into session July 26th. On the 26th day of July, which out in Missouri we call 'Turnip Day,' I am going to call Congress back and ask them to pass laws to halt rising prices, to meet the housing crisis—which they are saying they are for in their platform. At the same time I shall ask them to act upon other vitally needed measures." Truman had prepared carefully in laying this trap and he publicly predicted that the Eightieth Congress would not be up to the challenge:

> Now, my friends, if there is any reality behind that Republican platform, we ought to get some action from a short session of the 80th Congress. They can do this job in 15 days, if they want to do it. They will still have time to go out and run for office.
>
> They are going to try to dodge their responsibility. They are going to drag all the red herrings they can across this campaign, but I am here to say that Senator Barkley and I are not going to let them get away with it.

Now, what that worst 80th Congress does in this special session will be the test. The American people will not decide by listening to mere words, or by reading a mere platform. They will decide on the record, the record as it has been written. And in the record is the stark truth, that the battle lines of 1948 are the same as they were in 1932, when the Nation lay prostrate and helpless as a result of Republican misrule and inaction.

Whether the battle lines were the same in 1932 as in 1948 or not, it was clear that this president would employ the 1948 campaign to argue as if they were. In his wind-up, the president echoed Franklin Delano Roosevelt's words when he accepted his nomination in Chicago in 1932: "This is more than a political call to arms. Give me your help, not to win votes alone, but to win in this new crusade to keep America secure and safe for its own people." Truman concluded, "Now my friends, with the help of God and the wholehearted push which you can put behind this campaign, we can save this country from a continuation of the 80th Congress, and from misrule from now on. I must have your help. You must get in and push, and win this election. The country can't afford another Republican Congress."[12]

In his first act as the Democratic nominee, then, Harry S. Truman, invoking Depression-era fears and charges of Republican "misrule and inaction," challenged the Eightieth Republican Congress to go back into special session to pass the legislative proposals that had been endorsed in their own platform. While some felt the president's gesture was more of a political stunt than a sincere call to action, it was theatrical in a variety of senses, not the least of which was that it was dramatic in sweep and tone. As one reporter at the time noted, it was an "electrifying announcement" that put Truman "in an aggressive, attacking position, and until [the] Republicans get organized, the various congressional speakers will be speaking on many sectors instead of returning the assault as a unit."[13] This attempt to divide Republicans on the issues and, simultaneously, to take the heat off of himself was, politically, a rather brilliant stroke. The "do-nothing Congress" was a moniker that Truman felt would stick. In fact, he would use the fall whistle-stop train tour to continually tar and feather the Republicans with the ignominious label.

True to campaign strategy, Truman was quite content to battle Congress rather than Governor Dewey and leave it to Dewey either to defend his colleagues against Truman's charges or remain silent and risk appearing tepid in his support for his fellow Republicans.[14] The Truman forces had created a winning political strategy. Since the high-minded, unity-seeking (some might say unity-obsessed) governor was a frontrunner seeking, above all else, to avoid a fight or undue controversy, he seemed largely content to let Congress handle this newly created problem. Truman's tactic was abhorred and publicly denounced by the Republicans, and many felt they had good reason. This, too, was a development the president seems to have considered beforehand. Despite the polls, the president seemed to relish his political prospects. He felt that a combination of championing the people's interests while attacking an Eightieth Congress that subverted them at every turn was the best strategy for winning the White House and demonstrating his core values.[15]

Truman surprised the delegates with his call for a special session, and his confident tone put new resolve in the entire convention. Truman's strategy had been set forth in the Rowe-Clifford memorandum. In continuing to attack Congress and associate Dewey with congressional malfeasance, Truman had inaugurated a tactical rhetorical device that proved over time to be increasingly effective. Even as some quarters continued to roundly question and even bitterly complain about his "unfair" strategy, they were surprised at Truman's renewed gusto.

But neither the delegates in the convention hall that night nor those few who were awake enough in the wee hours to listen in on the radio felt Truman could actually win the 1948 election. While the convention address would give die-hard Democrats a glimmer of hope, placards displayed at the convention indicated that the president still had a long and treacherous political road ahead. One read: "We are mild about Harry." And the talk was that even though he landed the nomination, Truman was, in the parlance of the day, a "dead bird."

But engaged audiences inside and outside the hall heard a man with pluck and political savvy. Truman's 1948 nomination acceptance address "took the combative spirit of Theodore Roosevelt, combined it with FDR's contempt for sham," and inaugurated "his legendary 'give 'em hell' crusade." His image was more like "that of a banty-rooster or a scrappy flyweight fighter" than a confident incumbent president.[16] The lack of certainty in the upcoming election seemed to be an elixir that drove Truman to animated and sustained action. He seemed both ready and willing to meet the challenge of an uphill campaign.

Two days after the nomination acceptance address, the long-promised and long-feared Dixiecrat revolt was officially underway as Democrats from all over the South convened in Birmingham, Alabama, to attend to "states' rights." Governors Strom Thurmond and Fielding L. Wright would challenge Truman and Barkley and the traditional Democratic Party. This split was painful and it was significant. With Henry Wallace mounting a third-party attempt as well, this latest development threatened to siphon off votes for Truman.

Truman counted on his status in the African American community to help him overcome these rather ominous developments. On July 26, 1948, on the very day the president intended to recall Congress for the special session, Truman signed executive orders 9980 and 9981. The first addressed discrimination in federal employment, and the second, even more wide-reaching, called for the desegregation of U.S. armed forces. These two initiatives, enacted the summer before a critically important fall election campaign, helped assure the African American community that Truman was serious in his determination to address the social and political injustices he had identified in his landmark February 2, 1948, civil rights address. Signing these two prominent executive orders immediately after the Democratic National Convention also served notice that Truman would be undeterred by the Dixiecrat revolt. The symbolic and material effects of these actions cannot be dismissed lightly. The African American community could not help but note how decisively and concretely Truman had backed up his rhetoric with these two impressive executive orders.[17]

Truman gambled that Congress would not be receptive to his legislation and even calculated that if little was done in the special session he would derive a significant campaign issue. If the Eightieth Congress did not deliver on his wish list, he could single out a "do-nothing" Congress with even more just cause than before and hand the Republican nominee a difficult dilemma. After two weeks, Congress adjourned from the special session without having accomplished much. The Turnip Day session had "ground through eleven querulous days to a barren end."[18] Truman, true to his rhetorical instincts and his political strategy, immediately attacked the special session as a "failure."[19] The president would exploit the outcome unmercifully in his fall campaign.

The Fall Campaign Begins, September 1948

Truman designed a plan modeled after the June western train trip that he felt would help him win the campaign and preserve his principles. He would hold rallies in the large cities and make whistle-stops on the way to those larger destinations. It was an effort to build a coalition that could help diffuse the twin threats posed by the Dixiecrats and the Wallaceites, while simultaneously overcoming the almost universally held opinion that his Republican opponent, Thomas E. Dewey, was on the brink of becoming the next president of the United States. Truman made six trips from Washington to try to overcome the view of both the press and the pollsters that he had little chance of winning the 1948 election. Truman's strategy was not without a host of detractors; few believed that he would be able to change the outcome of the election. And while the plan to barnstorm the country by train promised to draw crowds curious to see the president along the designated whistle-stops, most everyone felt that Truman's ultimate defeat was a fait accompli. On the other hand, one could not totally discount an improbable outcome. As a *Washington Star* editorial observed presciently, "This [strategy] may prove to be more effective than most experts suppose. The American people like a fighter and tend to sympathize with the underdog, both of which Mr. Truman is."[1]

A Daunting Itinerary

September and October, of course, are key campaign months and Truman decided to take full advantage of the crucial time left prior to the election. The planned trip would be grueling for a man half his age. Even at age 64, the president relished the thought of getting his message out to the people. In September, Truman took to the rails with gusto and an air of confidence that few in his entourage shared. Indeed, while the polls seemed to indicate that he was on a futile run, Truman seemed to gain energy from every whistle-stop, and his enthusiasm seemed unquenchable.

The president would inaugurate his whistle-stop train tour with a visit to Michigan and a major speech to open the campaign at Cadillac Square in Detroit on Labor Day. He moved from Michigan to Ohio and then returned to Washington. On September 17, Truman embarked on a major western tour, beginning with stops at Pittsburgh, Pennsylvania and Crestline, Ohio. On September 18 he paused at Rock Island, Illinois, and then went on to Iowa where he made brief speeches at Davenport, Iowa City, Oxford, Grinnell, made a major speech at Dexter, and continued with whistle-stops at Des Moines, Melcher, and Chariton, as well as Trenton and Polo, Missouri. On September 19, Truman made three stops in Kansas; on September 20, he delivered a major speech in Denver, Colorado, and delivered four minor speeches as he made his way across the state. He finished his visit to Colorado on September 21 and moved on to Utah where he made a number of whistle-stops and delivered a major address in Salt Lake City. On September 22, he made stops in Nevada and California with major speeches in the latter state at Oakland on September 22 and Los Angeles on September 23. On September 24, Truman continued through California and went on to Arizona, where he delivered a major speech in Phoenix; he then traveled to New Mexico on September 25. The president continued on to Texas where he spent time September 25 through 28 delivering major speeches in El Paso and Bonham. From September 28 through October 1, Truman barnstormed through Oklahoma, Missouri,

Illinois, Indiana, Kentucky, and West Virginia. Major speeches were delivered in Tulsa, Carbondale, Louisville, and Charleston.[2]

Not since before World War II had a president employed the heart of the campaign season to go out into the cities, towns, and hamlets to greet the American people in person. Communities vied to be listed as a train stop on the president's itinerary, and when they learned they were not selected, because of time constraints or other political considerations, they expressed their disappointment quite vocally. In those places chosen for a presidential visit, the local communities, along with the president's advance men, made sure that the president was met with enthusiasm at each stop. All the staple political accouterments befitting a symbolic environment striking up an old-fashioned campaign tradition were conspicuously in evidence.

The train stops featured local brass bands that greeted Truman with "Hail to the Chief" or the "Missouri Waltz" or, in Indiana, "On the Banks of the Wabash." Children squealed in delight, held high from the outstretched arms of parents hoping to give their child get a better view of the commander-in-chief and expose them to an exciting sliver of shared history. At various and sundry stops, day or night, men, women, and children could be seen waving flags, hoisting placards, and waving happily. The red, white, and blue bunting that adorned the waiting areas had been carefully prepared and put into place ahead of time, and these preparations were repeated again and again for the next hamlet, town, or city.

As they made their way from the train stations to the larger cities, the president's motorcades were often accompanied with the music of marching bands as confetti and tape floated down in colorful sprays from the office building windows above. A typical motorcade would include four city police motorcycle escorts heading the motorcade followed by a Democratic Committee car, a lead car with secret service and police, the president's car with local dignitaries and secret service aboard, followed by another secret service car, news services in a separate car, and, finally, buses that might carry thirty or more additional passengers. In Pittsburgh, for example, there were thirty-three cars in all. The motorcade was protected in the rear by a police car with city and county officers on board. When Bess and Margaret made the trip to town, they often traveled in a separate car from that of the president. This was done as an additional security measure.[3]

When the president arrived for a major address, he was always introduced by local and state politicians and dignitaries and, more often than not, given a rousing musical welcome. Harry S. Truman truly enjoyed the hoopla. His wide grin may have hidden any rigors he was feeling on the campaign trail; each new crowd he met seemed to reinvigorate him. The president dutifully discussed the key political issues, but he also contentedly conjured up narratives of the past, weaving his own story with those of the people he visited, reflecting and embodying both the small-town and big city tales that made up a composite quilt of a uniquely stitched and colorfully blended American experience. Many times, the president was presented with a unique gift that embroidered him into the fabric of the particular place he visited; he accepted these gifts with graciousness and good humor. Often, just before the warning signal that it was time to push off for the next destination, Truman would lean over the back platform to shake hands and greet well-wishers until the warning signal sounded indicating it was time for the train to pull away. This last image of the president provides a snapshot of a time that seems long past.

Speechwriting Process
SPEECHWRITING TEAM

Clark Clifford headed Truman's speechwriting team for four years. Clifford contributed to many of the major addresses during the 1948 campaign. William "Bill" Batt coordinated a six-person team at the Democratic National Committee campaign headquarters, which was responsible for providing background research and suggested topics for the whistle-stop speeches. Charles S. Murphy, who served as an administrative assistant, began the 1948 campaign working with the Democratic National Committee on background work for the speeches Truman employed at the whistle-stops. Later, Murphy joined the speechwriters who traveled on the train. David D. Lloyd also worked for the DNC on the background for the Truman campaign speeches. George M. Elsey researched and helped draft the outlines for the whistle-stop remarks. Others included David E. Bell and David H. Stowe. In the final months of the whistle-stop tour, John Franklin Carter (whose pen name sometimes appeared as Jay Franklin) was invited on board the train. Samuel Rosenman, a holdover from the Roosevelt era, helped draft the 1948 convention address, and drafted some of the major addresses along the campaign trail. The president invited David Noyes and Bill Hillman to help draft campaign speeches as well. Hillman, in turn, asked Albert Z. (Bob) Carr to join the team. Finally, presidential press secretary Charles G. Ross and presidential appointments secretary Matthew Connelly often huddled on the train to ensure appropriate uptake on last-minute revisions to speeches or to smooth preparations for one particular stop or another.[4]

FORMS OF ADDRESS

The whistle-stop train tour provided the occasion for the president to deliver principally three types of speeches: major addresses in large cities, brief remarks delivered from the back platform of his personal train car, the *Ferdinand Magellan,* and minor speeches scheduled for delivery in designated cities and towns, which the president would often visit by motorcade after departing from a particular train stop. The president delivered twenty-six major addresses during the campaign. With the exception of those given at Detroit, Dexter, Denver, Oklahoma City, Miami, and Raleigh, the major speeches were all given at night and had fairly broad radio coverage. The major addresses featured key campaign issues intended for "nationwide consumption." Examples include a focus on labor in Detroit and Akron; farm issues in Dexter and Springfield; western development in Denver, Salt Lake City, and Oakland; Third Party candidacies and communism in Los Angeles, Oklahoma City, and Boston; atomic energy in Milwaukee; and foreign affairs in Miami and Brooklyn. These addresses were delivered largely by reading the manuscript of a prepared text. With few exceptions, major addresses did not contain large portions of extemporaneous remarks.

The back-platform remarks became known as the famous "whistle-stop" speeches. The "whistle stops" were delivered in small towns ranging from less than five hundred people to stops in cities that might have populations of half a million or more. Designed to be delivered extemporaneously, they generally lasted from two to fifteen minutes and could be delivered as early as six in the morning and as late as midnight on any particular day. A few days stretched even longer. The back-platform speeches were meant to increase enthusiasm for the president along the campaign tour, establish his key differences in policy with his opponents, and promote the major addresses he had planned for the large cities. From the president's point of view, the most important objective was to bring the campaign to the people whom he trusted to vote in his favor; he firmly believed that a vote for him was in their best interests. Truman also engaged in other minor speeches delivered after being driven by motorcade to a platform or makeshift stage with a podium that had been constructed for his appearance in that particular town or city.

SPEECH PREPARATION

According to Murphy, initially "[i]t turned out to be my responsibility to get the material out to the train. This included usually a draft of one major speech a day. And this was a very large undertaking for a small group to do and so the Research Division [located in Washington, D.C.] and its material were quite helpful." At times, people on board the train were responsible for turning out one major speech a day and a number of "smaller speeches at the same time." For major speeches, "The pattern that evolved was that we would send a draft of a speech from here [Washington] at night, it would be flown by courier plane that would land wherever that train was before day in the morning and they would put it on the train and Clifford would get it and start to work with the President on it on the train until they had what the President wanted, and they usually used it that night." Murphy joined the entourage on the train during the last ten days of the campaign.

Elsey was responsible for working up notes, texts, and outlines for the whistle-stop speeches. According to Murphy, "The pattern was that they would borrow material, a few facts from the draft of a major speech for that day and talk on the same topic, and used it along with local references, references that were of local interest to the people who might be there. And Elsey did a prodigious job on that, and I have never, never understood how he could do all that."

Murphy detailed the benefits that accrued from employing a working outline for the president's back-platform remarks: "We suggested it to him because we were searching for some method that would facilitate his saying what he had to say, so that he could come through." The idea was to "develop an outline that the President could use which would make sense grammatically if he did nothing but read it, that would be the bare bones of the speech." He could depart from it readily whenever he wished to and return to it at will. Frequently, although these outlines were prepared, "he used them not at all." In addition, "He didn't have time between stops and think about what he would say at the next stop, because between stops, he had to do other things, to talk with other people. And sometimes when he was suddenly called on to go out on the back platform and make a speech, something would occur to him readily, he could open his book; he could look and see what notes he had and this would remind him of something he would like to say." Certainly, "One of his favorite means of getting into a speech was to talk about the crowd some. It worked very well, almost always."

The president's own contributions to the speech drafting process are not to be dismissed. According to Murphy, in preparing for the next whistle-stop the president would "get the transcript of what he actually said in other whistle-stop speeches and put [some of the remarks] into later ones. So in this sense, I suppose he did more in writing his own whistle-stop speeches than anyone else because this was a standard technique."[5] This kind of editing also enabled the president to incorporate lines that had worked well elsewhere while incorporating a method of standardization that was well-tested.

The brief outlines utilized by the president for the whistle-stop speeches included introductory material that would identify local politicians and candidates, pertinent landmarks, industries, and/or projects, and key issues identified for presidential comment at that particular stop, such as labor, high prices, housing, or other pertinent issues directly affecting the city, town, or region. Sometimes additional background material would be attached to the speech outlines for the president's use. Suggested concluding remarks would invariably reinforce the notion that the stakes were both personal and high. Truman told his audiences in no uncertain terms that the election should be interpreted as a "fight between the people and the Special Interests." He continually warned, "if you don't want to make things still worse, you had better be sure that this time [unlike the 1946 midterm elections] all of you get out and vote."[6]

Johannes Hoeber, a member of the DNC research support team, indicates that the whistle-stop venues were given the following attention by support staff: "We did two things. We wrote a one-page backgrounder on the nature of the whistle-stop city, its socio-economic structure, its politics, its prior political record, and who the key people were in that particular area. And then we attached . . . to it regular drafts, very brief drafts, a page, two pages, three pages, double-spaced. But they were regular speech drafts." Hoeber added, "If there was a major Truman speech coming up somebody from the Research Division went to that place for a couple of days to kind of savor the local flavor as background material."[7]

Elsey wrote Murphy to comment on the utility of the outlines supplied by the DNC research team: "Batt['s] outlines are very helpful. I usually use them as the basis for an outline which is handed to the President. *Sometimes* he follows the outline, but whether he does or not, he expects one for each stop and wants one. Pray for us."[8] The drafted material was intended to serve as a back-up for the president: sometimes he chose to employ a good part of the material, sometimes he used just a little, and sometimes he ignored the outlines entirely.

According to Ross, on major speeches the president "went over every line with his staff, and worked painstakingly on draft after draft." Ross credited Clifford with "most of the work." Elsey, who served as Clifford's assistant, "worked long hours on notes for the whistle-stop talks." Ross testifies that the speechwriters accompanying the president on the train were a tight-knit, selfless, sometimes contentious lot: "We had our speech-revising sessions around the table in the little dining room of the President's private car. Generally there were Clifford, Murphy, the politically wise Connelly, and myself. Nobody had any special pride of authorship, but we did get into heated arguments now and then. The president would grin and say 'All right, you fellows fight it out and I'll decide.' He never lost his good temper, although we gave him plenty of provocation." The pressure was palpable: "We were operating just one jump ahead of he sheriff" since "many of the speeches were written as we went along."[9]

Method of Rhetorical Analysis

Truman's whistle-stop campaign owed a great deal of its success to the president's penchant for launching and sustaining populist appeals. Major addresses, minor speeches, and back-of-the-train-platform remarks all reflected Truman's unique application of populist persuasion. Before turning to an analysis and evaluation of the formal fall campaign and the public address associated with Truman's whistle-stop train tour, it is necessary to illuminate briefly the historical and political roots of populism, identify characteristic populist rhetorical strategies, and situate Truman's campaign discourse in the populist tradition. This brief discussion will help structure and amplify a key argument advanced in this study.

Populism

At the end of the nineteenth century, the farmers and laborers who joined the populist movement formed an alliance in the rural heartland, the West and the South. Together they posed one primary question: "Why were so many Americans desperately poor while a handful grew fabulously wealthy?" Combining a penchant for Jacksonian anti-monopolism and old-fashioned social reform, theirs was a distinctly American reading of cultural history and social egalitarianism. In the 1890s, in particular, they advocated the idea "that in an advanced urban-industrial society the federal government has a role to play in cushioning the impact of economic collapse and in restoring and maintaining prosperity." Populist platforms depicted "a nation brought to the verge of moral, political, and material ruin" and "outlined a program of governmental action to curtail the special privileges of the wealthy and protect the equal rights of working people."[10]

Michael Kazin argues that populists "conceive of ordinary people as a noble assemblage not bound narrowly by class, view their elite opponents as self-serving and undemocratic and seek to mobilize the former against the latter."[11] Representing neither the poor nor the rich, populist rhetors seek to unify the vast majority of Americans who find themselves in the middle. Thus, "yeoman farmers, urban craftsmen, native-born factory workers, [and] homeowners struggling to pay their taxes" are the very citizens to whom populist appeals are targeted.[12] Populist arguments are most effective when "the people who are the target audience . . . feel powerless and resentful toward an elite that is perceived as unresponsive to their needs."[13]

Kazin maintains that populist rhetoric typically relies on four characteristic themes: majority rule, a producer ethic, opposition to the elite, and a restoration of national ideals. Majority rule speaks to the principle of acting in conformance with the social, moral, and political will of the people. The producer ethic places its trust in those individuals who have actually created the wealth from their industriousness and heavy labor. The common laborers are on the front lines of the nation's productivity and are therefore the presumed guarantors of our freedoms and those most suited to protect and defend our national interests. They are the keepers of the flame of civic duty and piety. The anti-elitist stance particularly regards special interests as inimical to the national interest and remains wary of the wealth and privilege that those special interests serve, whether these encroachments come from the government, industry, or big business. There is usually a demand that people rise up and protect their interests. This is often accompanied by a call for a movement to restore the people's rightful place in the American hierarchy. A return to common values and ideals and to the protection of the ordinary citizen is presumed necessary to achieve balance, enable virtue, and restore justice in the land.[14]

Since populist leaders rise to the defense of the people whose lives and livelihood seem ever prone to attack, it is incumbent on the populist political leader to demonstrate not only that he or she can refocus ideals and defend them from unscrupulous attack but also design and implement policies and deliver programs consonant with the people's mandate. Thus, the populist politician must establish consistency between proposed policies and programs and professed ideals. This is the constant measurement by which the populist politician is evaluated by engaged audiences. Given these particular predilections, the populist rhetor is prone to glorification of the "common man," which, in turn, may polarize the electorate.[15]

In pitting elite powerful forces against the "common" man or woman, populist rhetors can polarize people precisely because their arguments seem based on class divisions; typically, their scapegoats are the rich and powerful elite. In fact, one rhetorical scholar has indicated that anti-elitism "is the very core of populism."[16] Rhetorically, special interests, monopolies, Wall Street, and big business all become targets of opprobrium precisely because individual and group self-interest is portrayed as overcoming the public good in political society, not only making things harder for ordinary citizens but also upsetting a sacrosanct shared American value hierarchy of civic virtue and replacing it with greed, ostentatious displays of misbegotten wealth for a fortunate few, and a disregard, if not disdain, for the misfortunate but hard-working majority.

It is hardly surprising, then, that populist speakers are often labeled "demagogues" because their discourse agitates their audiences and may stir proponents and opponents into an emotional frenzy. Demagoguery, however, is in the eye of the beholder. It may be nothing more than a label one pins on one's political opponents.[17] As Hogan and Williams have argued, referring to a politician as a "demagogue" may merely reflect one's own "prejudice," and even "an intellectual aversion to . . . [an] indecorous, vituperative, and revivalistic brand of democratic populism."[18] Moreover, use of the term, at a minimum, may "oversimplify" a complex political activity and may actually reveal how one "take[s] sides in the perennial class struggle between the 'haves' and the 'have nots.'"[19] Given that Truman employed a populist discourse in the 1948 campaign and that he was also upon occasion accused of demagoguery, this study will speak to this issue and offer a summary judgment.

Truman's background as a farmer, small businessman, veteran, mason, and county judge, among other experiences, gave him a good sense of the norms and values as well as the successes and failures of the "producing classes." The president's rhetorical identification is certainly clear. As Robert Underhill observes, "Truman came out of the Midwest at midcentury and represented a twentieth century version of Populism. He was against big business, Wall Street, and the railroads. He used words and phrases gleaned from Teddy Roosevelt, George Norris, and William Jennings Bryan."[20] What is interesting about Truman in 1948 is that he mixed the politician's intuitive pragmatic sense of how to be successful with voters by building a coalition that would help him win in raw numbers with a progressive-minded homespun rhetoric tinged with an enduring populist appeal. The president's argument was premised as much on what the common citizen could lose in the 1948 election outcome as much as it was on what was to be gained by electing Harry Truman president. Truman could promise continued prosperity for the people and point to a Democratic New Deal tradition of serving the people's interests. In electing Dewey and endorsing Republicans, Truman indicated that much would be lost and even more would be threatened. He pointed to a slippery slope of a reduced quality of life for ordinary Americans that made voting for the opposing party seem particularly risky, if not foolhardy.

In essence, the president set out to prove to the American people that he was the man best qualified to defend the national interest. He wrapped his discourse in a populist patina of civic-minded education. By September of 1948, Truman had found ample time for testing his political strategy and his newly minted extemporaneous rhetorical prowess. It was time to begin the campaign in earnest. While Truman may have opposed the railroads as one of industry's most elite and egregious monopolies, he would take to the rails as the best platform to mount his rhetorical crusade on behalf of the people. Rhetorically, during the fall campaign, Truman emphasized the following generic populist themes: (1) he alone could best represent the will of the people; (2) he had abiding trust in and looked out for those who labored to produce America's wealth; (3) he stood against elitist and special interests inimical to the common good; and (4) he represented the political party that was best equipped to honor the ideals of and keep the ordinary citizen's place in the American value hierarchy and extend the prosperity he or she enjoyed now and could anticipate in the future. These bedrock populist rhetorical appeals were crucial to forging the necessary coalition first articulated in the Rowe-Clifford memorandum as pivotal to a successful bid for the presidency in the 1948 election.

Labor Day Speech

The president's first campaign swing was targeted at Michigan and Ohio. He left Washington, D.C., at 3:30 PM on September 5 and formally opened his campaign on September 6 with a nationally broadcast Labor Day address at 1:30 P.M., EDT, in Detroit's Cadillac Square. Flanked by Walter P. Reuther, president of the United Automobile Workers (CIO) and Frank X. Martel, head of the American Federation of Labor (AFL) in Detroit, each of whom publicly pledged their support, Truman gathered his thoughts and his composure and began to address a huge throng estimated at 175,000 people.[21]

After praising the labor leaders for their solidarity in support of his election bid, the president engaged in a bit of fear-mongering: "These are critical times for labor and for all who work. There is great danger ahead. Right now, the whole future of labor is wrapped up in one simple proposition. If, in this next election, you get a Congress and an administration friendly to labor, you have much to hope for. If you get an administration and a Congress unfriendly to labor, you have much to fear, and you had better look out." The "spokesmen of reaction" were associated with the "Republican 80th Congress," which, having taken power two years earlier, "promptly fell into the familiar Republican pattern of aid for big business and attack on labor." Truman charged, "The Republicans promptly voted themselves a cut in taxes and voted you a cut in freedom. That 80th Republican Congress failed to crack down on prices but it cracked down on labor all right!"

Truman next decried the Taft-Hartley Act as one the Republicans enacted over his veto, placing "a dangerous weapon into the hands of the big corporations."[22] He argued that "labor is just beginning to feel the effects of the Taft-Hartley law. And you and I know that the Taft-Hartley law is only a foretaste of what you will get if the Republican reaction is allowed to continue to grow." Even as he spoke, Truman charged, "the Republicans in Congress are preparing further and stronger measures against labor." Having threatened his labor union audience with dark Republican intentions toward future policy initiatives, Truman expanded his target audience: "Not only the labor unions, but all men and women who work are in danger, and the danger is greatest for those who do not belong to unions. If anything, the blows will fall most severely on the white-collar workers and the unorganized workers. And that is not all!" If voters in 1948 allowed "a reactionary Republican administration" to once again take office, it seemed certain they could bring with them "another 'boom and bust' cycle," just as before. Terming this set of dire circumstances "an exceedingly real possibility," Truman warned, "You can already see signs of it. The 'boom' is on for them, and the 'bust' has begun for you." While such an aphorism may have struck a chord, Truman went even further. He argued that in the future the only way to keep prosperity going was to open new relationships and engage in joint actions: "I think it is clear that labor will need to link its position more closely with that of the farmers and the small businessman." Since these were three primary target groups Truman needed for his own election, attempts to unify their interests served the president's as well.

Inflation was a key issue that tied most working Americans together. The president linked perceptively the rights of unions to the right to support and sustain one's family: "It is not only the rights of the unions which are at stake, but the standard of living of your families. . . . My sympathy is with those best of business managers—the wives and mothers of this Nation. Think how they have made the pay envelope stretch with each rise in prices." The blame for the predicament was placed directly at his opponents' doorstep: "Now, Mother has to outfit the children for school at outrageous prices. How she does it, I don't know. I tried to help her out in this terrible price situation, but I got absolutely no help from that 'do-nothing' 80th Republican Congress." Truman portrayed this sorry set of circumstances as one threatening the nation's quality of life, if not liberty itself: "Make no mistake, you are face to face with a struggle to preserve the very foundations of your rights and your standards of living." Truman rhetorically positioned himself as the only man in America who could stop the insidious Republican juggernaut.

In trying to unify key coalitions, the president's appeals on behalf of common working people had not only implied that he would look out for those who labored in America but that he and his party were the *only ones* interested in doing so. Sometimes this took a turn that invoked stereotypes, if not outright class divisions: "Today, too many Americans in dining cars, in country clubs, and fashionable resorts are repeating, like parrots, the phrase 'labor must be kept in its place.' It is time that all Americans realized that the place of labor is side by side with the businessman and with the farmer and not one degree lower." The president was not above striking a conspiratorial tone. "Remember," he said, "that the reactionary of today is a shrewd man. . . . He is a man with a calculating machine where his heart ought to be. He has learned a great deal about how to get his way by observing demagogues and reactionaries in other countries. And now he has many able allies in the press and in the radio." This seemed a vague reference to his opponent, who was known for a kind of cool, calculating "efficiency." To be sure, no one ever accused Thomas E. Dewey of being warm-hearted. But by vaguely associating him with "demagogues and reactionaries"—perhaps even the Hitlers and the Mussolinis of the world—Truman appeared to have crossed the line. Would-be critics, and even some sympathizers, fretted that this kind of rhetoric bordered on demagoguery. In this instance, it seemed like Truman had overreached. One could well imagine that the press in America, labeled as "able allies" of the "shrewd men," would be quite sensitive to the harshness in his words.

But the labor audience in Detroit appreciated the blunt talk and identified with the descriptions of a dire state of affairs. Truman drove the point home: "All of labor stands at the crossroads today. You can elect a reactionary administration. You can elect a Congress and an administration which stands ready to play fair with every element in American life and enter a new period of hope. The choice is yours." In concluding his speech, Truman, in full knowledge that the 1946 midterm elections had yielded a less than stellar turnout of his normal constituents, tried to rally the forces to vote: "Labor has always had to fight for its gains. Now you are fighting for the whole future of the labor movement. We are in a hard, tough fight against shrewd and rich opponents. They know they can't count on your vote. Their only hope is that you won't vote at all. They have misjudged you. I know that we are going to win this crusade for the right!"[23] Truman had launched his campaign with an appeal to a key political constituency, one that he would address repeatedly and emphatically throughout the remainder of the campaign. In this campaign kick-off address, we receive a clear picture of Truman's general rhetorical strategy. He would rely on tried and true old-fashioned populist appeals by defending the ordinary citizen, critiquing the policies driven by the special interests represented by the "shrewd men" whom he associated with his Republican opponents, and adamantly portraying himself as protecting a "way of life" and a standard of living that most Americans identified with and revered. As he framed it rhetorically, the president was at the vanguard of both a political campaign *and* a moral crusade. It was not a prescription for the faint of heart. Press opinion scored the president for engaging in a bit of demagoguery and indicated that Truman's unrestrained speechifying did not bode well for the upcoming campaign.[24]

Dexter, Iowa

One important early campaign stop would be Dexter, Iowa, where Truman planned to deliver a major speech on farm issues. The president had received and accepted an invitation to speak at the National Plowing Match and Soil Conservation Field Day. This event was sponsored by a non-profit farming organization dedicated to soil conservation and better land use. The plowing match drew "40 champion plowmen" who competed for fifteen hundred dollars in prize money and a national title. Given good weather, planners expected to draw seventy-five thousand people, including some three hundred Flying Farmers. Arrangements were made to park thirty thousand automobiles. State Highway Patrol would provide security, and approximately thirty church groups and veterans' organizations made sure there would be enough food. Plans were also made to conduct a "parade of farm progress" and to crown a "Plowman's Queen" to highlight the festivities.[25]

One key political development would prove pivotal to the Dexter address. New Deal legislation had created government price supports ensuring farmers a basic payment for their crops. If the market price was higher than the support price, farmers sold their corn and wheat directly to the commercial market. If the market price was below the government support level, farmers could obtain loans based on the government's guaranteed price and then sell the crop when feasible and repay the loan. But loan eligibility was based on storage of the crop in a government-approved facility, which meant farmers had to locate and pay for a commercial storage bin or use one provided by the Commodity Credit Corporation (CCC). At the end of the war the CCC had cut back the available storage space rather severely. The Republican-dominated House Banking and Currency Committee met to renew the CCC charter in mid-1948 and, in an act of near-sighted frugality, banned the CCC from acquiring more storage space. This proved unfortunate for farmers, since 1948 yielded an historic bumper crop; corn was harvested at an all-time high, and the wheat crop came in as the second largest in the nation's history. This abundance meant that corn and wheat prices had fallen dramatically, and the farmers were looking frantically for storage space. The Republicans blamed the Democrats and the Democrats blamed the Republicans. Regardless of responsibility, grain prices continued to plummet.[26] Before the scheduled speech, Connelly furnished Truman "a reminder from Secretary Brannan about the bins." Farm prices reinforced the political opportunity given to the president by the bin shortage: "The grain harvest that year was huge, causing market prices to tumble: corn dropped from $2.46 a bushel in January to $1.21 in November, parity support was $1.53, and with no bins farmers could not collect parity payments."[27]

Truman felt confident he could convince his fellow midwestern farmers of the need for support. Stepping up to a bevy of microphones with a flower in his lapel and wearing sunglasses to cut the glare from a burning afternoon sun, the president readied himself on the makeshift platform to deliver a prepared text. He greeted the farmers warmly: "It does my heart good to see the grain fields of the Nation again. They are a wonderful sight. The record-breaking harvests you have been getting in recent years have been a blessing. Millions of people have been saved from starvation by the food you have produced. The whole world has reason to be everlastingly grateful to the farmers of the United States." He flattered the farmers on their contribution to international stability: "In a very real sense, the abundant harvests of this country are helping to save the world from communism. Communism thrives on human misery. And the crops you are producing are driving back the tide of misery in many lands. Your farms are a vital element in America's foreign policy. Keep that in mind, that is of vital importance to us and to the world." The president was reassuring: "It is the policy of this Government to continue working for peace with every instrument at our command." But his appearance at Dexter would have little to do with foreign affairs, and everyone there knew it. Truman turned the discussion to continued prosperity and he connected that prosperity to the need for cooperation from some key groups, which happened to constitute the key constituencies he was courting for the election:

Will this Nation succeed in keeping its prosperity? Will it preserve its high standards of living next year, and the year after, and the year after that?

I know of only one way to get assured prosperity. That is by cooperation of agriculture with labor, cooperation of agriculture and labor with business, large and small.

When these groups work together in a common cause, this country can achieve miracles. We saw that during the war. We saw it before the war. By common effort, in the last 15 years, every group in the Nation steadily increased its income. Our people rose from despair to the highest living standards in the history of the world.

So long as the farmer, the worker, and the businessman pull together in the national interest, this country has everything to hope for.

This kind of solidarity with the "producing classes" certainly seemed to speak to populist aspirations, especially when juxtaposed with the president's caution that it would be "terribly dangerous" to "let one group share the Nation's policies in its own interest, at the expense of the others." The villains, of course, who had a history of this interest-begotten prejudicial power happened to be his erstwhile opponents: "That is what happened in the 1920s, under the big business rule of the Republicans. Those were the days when big corporations had things their own way. The policies that Wall Street big business wanted were the policies that the Republicans adopted. Agriculture, labor, and small business played second fiddle, while big business called the tune."

Having identified his target, Truman proceeded to lay into his opponents. Reminding his audience of the hard times associated with Republican rule, Truman recited a litany of unmitigated sorrows: "You remember the results of that Wall Street Republican policy. You remember the big boom and the great crash of 1929. You remember that in 1932 the position of the farmer had become so desperate that there was actual violence in many farming communities. You remember that insurance companies and banks took over much of the land of small independent farmers—223,000 farmers lost their farms. That was a painful lesson. It should not be forgotten for a moment." He repeated himself on these issues to drive home painful memories of misfortune: the depression of the 1930s, boom and bust cycles, farm prices at an all-time low. Truman contrasted the poor Republican record with that of the Democrats: "Since then the farmer has come a long way. The agricultural program of the Democratic administration in 16 years has enabled farmers to attain decent standards of living. Interest rates on farm credit have been sharply brought down. Farm mortgage indebtedness has been reduced by more than 50 percent. Farm mortgage foreclosures have almost disappeared. In 1947 the smallest number of farm foreclosures in the history of the country took place. All this was done under a Democratic administration."

As Truman portrayed it, there was a "great danger" that today's farmer "may be voted out of a fair deal, and into a Republican deal," a circumstance seemingly spawned by nefarious forces indeed: "The Wall Street reactionaries are not satisfied with being rich. They want to increase their power and their privileges, regardless of what happens to the other fellow. They are gluttons of privilege. These gluttons of privilege are now putting up fabulous sums of money to elect a Republican administration." These conspirators "expect a Republican administration to carry out their will, as it did in the days of Harding, Coolidge, and Hoover." Perhaps even more alarmingly, "Republican reactionaries want an administration that will assure privilege for big business, regardless of what may happen to the rest of the Nation. The Republican strategy is to divide the farmer and the industrial worker—to get them to squabbling with each other—so that big business can grasp the balance of power and take the country over, lock, stock, and barrel. To gain this end, they will stop at nothing." And the president issued a graphic warning about continuing with the Republicans in power in the future: "What they have taken away from you thus far would only be an appetizer for the economic tapeworm of big business." The president supplied a ready antidote: "Your best protection is to elect a Democratic Congress that will play fair with the farmer."

"Gluttons of privilege" who had become so surfeited that they had developed an "economic tapeworm," of course, graphically suggested an appetite that was clearly out of control. The idea that Republicans were conspiring with the wealthy to prop up "big business" without any regard for the farmer and the laborer tarnished his opponents as co-conspirators in a huge self-interested cabal.

Truman brought up the storage bins as proof that his opponents would "stop at nothing." He began his verbal assault with another graphic, almost gruesome, metaphor: "This Republican Congress has already stuck a pitchfork in the farmer's back. They have already done their best to keep the price supports from working. Many growers have sold wheat this summer at less than the support price, because they could not find proper storage. When the Democratic administration had to face this problem in the past, the Government set up grain bins all over the wheat and corn belts to provide storage." Once again, the people responsible for the perfidy were readily identified: "These big-business lobbyists and speculators persuaded the Congress not to provide the storage bins for the farmers. They tied the hands of the administration. They are preventing us from setting up storage bins that you will need in order to get the support price for your grain." Moreover, it was "this same Republican 80th Congress that gave the speculative grain trade a rake-off at your expense." After launching this fusillade, Truman posed a simple, direct, and, in the context of what he was saying, compellingly reasonable question targeted directly to this audience: "I wonder how many times you have to be hit on the head before you find out who's hitting you? It's about time that the people of America realized what the Republicans have been doing to them."

Truman adopts a role here as educator-in-chief. Not only is this in line with the long tradition of populist orators, but the lesson is made more palatable by the simple, direct idiom used in the telling. In essence, Truman appeals to common sense and self-interest. Even when Truman takes pains to deny Republican charges, it is delivered with a grassroots mentality and is likely to contain an aphorism or two to ensure his narrative denial fully registers: "Republicans are telling the farmers that the high cost of manufactured goods on the farm is due to this Government's labor policy. That's plain hokum. It's an old political trick. 'If you can't convince 'em, confuse 'em.' But this time it won't work."

Truman's Dexter message can be summed up in these two passages: "Wall Street expects its money this year to elect a Republican administration that will listen to the gluttons of privilege first, and to the people not at all." In contrast, "The Democratic Party represents the people. It is pledged to work for agriculture. It is pledged to work for labor. It is pledged to work for the small businessman and the white-collar worker. The Democratic Party puts human rights and human welfare first." In concluding his address, Truman pleads: "I'm not asking you just to vote for me. Vote for yourselves! Vote for your farms! Vote for the standard of living that you have won under a Democratic administration! Get out there on election day, and vote for your future!"[28] The response to the Dexter speech was polite but not overly demonstrative. Truman was not particularly concerned about this response because it was typical of his experience with farmers.

Robert J. Donovan, who covered the campaign, judged that the Dexter address, with its multiple unrestrained passages, was something unique and echoed an earlier era. Truman's rhetorical scorched-earth strategy against the Republicans seemed a bit over the top, if not overtly unfair. Donovan complained of Truman, "Any charge that came into his head . . . he flung without compunction at the Republicans." The president's opponents never answered his charges: "No nationally heard voice was raised against his tirades about Republican servitude to big business."[29] Clifford, reflecting later on the Dexter address, seems to have had a few misgivings but certainly not enough to cause him any undue regret. Clifford felt the speech was "effective" because it demonstrated to "voters that Harry Truman was a fighter, not a quitter, and it raised serious concerns about the policies the Republicans would follow if they recaptured the White House."[30] Truman left Dexter secure in his belief that he had won the farmers' allegiance.

After Dexter, Truman continued the fall western tour. He went on to Missouri, Kansas, Colorado, Utah, Nevada, and California. On his return trip from the West, the president stopped in Arizona, New

Mexico, Texas, Oklahoma, Missouri, Illinois, Indiana, Kentucky, and West Virginia. Truman's back-platform addresses in California serve as excellent exemplars of Truman's emerging speaking style at the western whistle-stops.

In California, Truman used the local and regional issues to attack the Eightieth Congress. He targeted key western interests like irrigation and reclamation, waterpower, housing, and farm support. At his stop in Oceanside, Truman lambasted the Republicans: "The Democratic Party has been responsible for the development of water power, and the other things in which the West is vitally interested. If you read the record, you will find that all these great projects originated under Democratic administrations, and you will find that this Republican 80th Congress has done everything it possibly can to sabotage the West. And they are still at it. You can't afford to allow that to happen." Truman also blamed his opponents for the housing shortage: "You are interested in housing. The Republican Congress sabotaged the housing bill. That bill passed the Senate and went over to the House, and the Chairman of the Banking and Currency Committee and the Chairman of the Rules Committee prevented the House from voting on that measure. I am sure that the House, if it had been allowed to vote by the Republican leadership, would have passed that [Wagner-Ellender-Taft] housing bill. . . . Senator Taft himself helped to kill that bill—his own bill with his name on it." Truman issued a direct warning: "If you send another Congress back there with a Republican tinge and a Republican majority, you will have the same old bunch of mossbacks in charge that are in charge now, and you won't get a thing."

After promising a brighter future with the Democrats, in stark contrast to the regressive Republican record of the past, Truman called upon his audience to act: "Now, it is up to you to decide whether you want to turn the clock back and leave the saboteurs in the Congress or whether you want to go forward with the Democratic Party and accomplish what is necessary to make this country great." Participation in the national election would be the key: "If you don't go out and vote the 2nd of November, and you have this backward-looking outfit in complete control of the Government, then you won't have anybody to blame but yourselves. If you do go out and vote, as I am sure you are going to, I am not going to worry about the result, because the people know what is right. The people are usually right if they can get the facts—and I am trying to give them to you. That is the reason I came out here."[31] In referring to his opponents as "mossbacks," "saboteurs," and "backward-looking," Truman's oratory seemed a bit demagogic to some, but the labels helped Truman drive home his charges that the Republicans represented the politics of the past and that their policies subverted the common interest.

Truman employed his major speeches and whistle-stop remarks not only to attack his Republican opponents but also to support local Democratic candidates and educate the nation's citizens on the specific issues he felt most affected their lives. A typical day of barnstorming in California provides a case in point. As Truman traveled across California's fertile valleys on September 23, his train stopped seven times for back-platform remarks. In Merced at 6:55 AM, the president observed, "I don't think the Republicans ever did anything specific for the farmer. If they did, it was by accident and not intention." The vote to be cast was obvious: "There is only one thing you can do to protect yourselves, and that is on the 2nd of November to go to the polls and vote for a Democratic Congressman. Mr. White, I think, is the candidate from this district, and they tell me that he is a fine man." Truman would inevitably include a bit of humor with his entreaties: "You ought to elect Mr. White to the Congress; and if you do that, of course, you will elect a Democratic President, and I won't be troubled with the housing shortage." The line about the "housing shortage" had by now become standard fare.

Truman was not afraid to invoke his work ethic, even if it was sometimes imperiled by his strenuous schedule. In Fresno at 8:12 AM, the president declared: "I was supposed to get up at 4 o'clock this morning for a bunch of people up here in Tracy at 5 o'clock, but I didn't make it! I was sorry about that, but then you know, a workhorse can do only so many hours in a day, and I skipped that one." Truman also built his ethos with his audience by sharing his hard-won credentials as a farmer and a veteran, experiences he employed as warrants for gaining their trust and addressing their problems: "I can remember very well, I ran a farm for the best 10 years of my life in Jackson County, Mo. It had 600 acres on it, and I went there when I was 22 years old and left it when I was 33 to go to war. I didn't claim any exemption on account of that farm, nor did I claim any exemption for being 33 years old. I went over and joined a battery of field artillery. There are a few fellows on this train that have been with me in that division. I am not bragging about that because that is just what I ought to have done, but I wanted to impress upon you that I know something about the farm situation." Truman, upon occasion, mercilessly pilloried his opponents in particular localities. Republican congressional representative Bertrand Gearhart, a member of the House Ways and Means Committee was one notable recipient of the president's ire: "You have got a terrible Congressman here in this district. He is one of the worst. He is one of the worst obstructionists in the Congress. He has done everything he possibly could to cut the throats of the farmer and the laboringman. If you send him back, that will be your fault if you get your own throat cut." Or, again, just as likely, the Republicans in general fell under the president's reproach:

> Now, you want to analyze this situation carefully and thoroughly. I am not asking you to vote for me alone. I want you to vote for yourselves. Vote for your own interests. Vote for the interests of the whole country.
>
> Of course if you are not interested in the interests of the whole country, then vote for these economic royalists and let them take you over. That is what they hope to do. This Republican 80th Congress is only the first step. It doesn't make any difference what they say they believe. Actions speak louder than words. What you need to do is understand what this 80th Congress did to the farmer and the laboringman and the white-collar worker, and you can't help but make your mind up in the right direction.

Use of the words "cutthroats" and "economic royalists" evoked populist themes in simple, easy-to-understand, graphic fashion. Such nomenclature gained attention and perhaps even a little admiration. For if one shuddered a bit at the style, there was no gainsaying the fact that the message was straightforward and the position it represented crystal clear.

At Tulare at 9:26 AM, he praised the fecundity of the land and those who tilled it:

> This valley, I am told, is one of the most diversified in the world—that you raise everything in this valley that goes to make life worthwhile in the world. Keep that up.
>
> In order to keep that up, you have got to have a Government that is in sympathy with what you are trying to do. You have got to have a Government that understands what it means to the everyday man to put the sweat of his brow into a piece of land.

He chided the assembly to do what it had not done in the midterm election: "In 1946 you didn't do your duty on election day. Two-thirds of you stayed at home. Two-thirds of you didn't vote, and one-third of the people in this United States voted in that awful 'do-nothing' 80th Congress—and look what you got." He again cautioned facetiously: "If you do that again you won't deserve any sympathy—not at all!" The line was used over and over again.

At Bakersfield at 10:50 AM, the president continued his barrage against the Republicans on issues vital to the region such as water and power: "The situation is such that if you don't watch your p's and q's, your valley is liable to be ruined. For years and years we have been endeavoring to implement a policy of water and power in this valley that would save it, due to the water table in this end of the valley going down. In order to do that, we have got to have people in the Congress and in the Government who are interested in the welfare of the people. You have had a sample of how the Republicans act when they get control of the Government." Truman posed as a man of the people who would continue a government of the people.

The president's next stop was Tehachapi, where he was greeted by a group of school children at 12:45 PM: "It is a pleasure to greet you. I am most happy to see all of you young people, and I appreciate your coming out to see the President. I wonder if you would like to see my wife and daughter? Here is the First Lady—she is the boss. And I will introduce her boss to you, Margaret. I want to compliment you young people; you are the most orderly bunch of young people I have seen on the whole trip." Margaret was particularly displeased with her father's appellation, "boss," but the children and the others who heard the introduction loved it.

At 1:30 PM the president pulled into Mohave. Here he distinguished between what he labeled "two theories of government in this country." He elaborated: "One theory believes that the special interests—that is, the people who have control of everything—should get all the profits and all the welfare of the country, and what little trickles down the other people can get by chance if they are there to get it." On the other hand, there is the theory "that there should be an equal distribution of the wealth. That is, the farmer should get his share, the laboringman should get his share, the white-collar man should get his, and the small businessman should get his." This latter theory was attributed to the Democrats and the former to the Republicans. Truman argued that the Republicans did not like the Democratic theory and that "this last 80th Republican Congress conclusively proved that when they get control of any part of the Government they work only for special interests." An equal distribution of the wealth contrasted directly with the wealth of those whose earnings were gained by privilege and special interest.

The president continued his populist appeals in Burbank at 4:25 PM. Not only did Truman pit special interests against that of the people, his polarizing campaign rhetoric portrayed the Republicans as a party of the past whose policies were inimical to prosperity: "The issues are clearly drawn in this campaign. It is the special interests against the people. The Republican 80th Congress proved conclusively that Republican policy has not changed one bit. They are just as they were in 1920, 1924, 1928, and 1932. They haven't changed a bit. This Congress tried its level best to turn the clock back, and if I had not been there standing in the way to protect you, they would have been a success in turning the clock way back." And Truman made sure he targeted the message to his key voting blocs: "They took a fall out of the farmer. They took a fall out of the laboringman. They took a fall out of business generally for the benefit of just a few."[32] The overall pattern and effect of such discourse at these train stops becomes apparent. The colloquialisms help drive the message home. The Republicans are "cutthroats" who will stop at nothing to "take a fall out of" farmers, laborers, and small business people. "Don't turn back the clock." If you do, you risk your own growth and prosperity: "If you don't watch your p's and q's, your valley is liable to be ruined." Citizens need to come forward and vote their interests, which are more than consonant with the national interest. In 1946, citizens avoided their "duty" and then "look what you got." Truman's homespun arguments could be adduced by both reason and common sense—and both reason and common sense dictated that voters cast their valued, even momentous vote for the president, for themselves, and for their country.

Following a long and exhausting day of speech-making and campaigning, the president traveled by motorcade to Gilmore Stadium in Los Angeles, where he was scheduled for a major address on domestic policy issues and his efforts for peace. The speech is significant for its major attack on Henry Wallace. Throughout the address, the president sought to reinforce the important stakes that the 1948 election outcome had in ensuring continued prosperity. In the analysis of this speech, particular attention will be paid to the two greatest campaign issues Truman had to address—the high cost of living and the fears of war. If the people could be assuaged on those two matters, Truman felt he had a fighting chance.

Gilmore Stadium, Los Angeles, September 23

All the glitz and glamour that Hollywood could muster seemed assembled for the president's appearance. Gilmore Stadium opened at six that evening. A disc jockey spun music until musicians from an American Legion Band began a live performance, followed by the Our Lady of Talpa Band. Soon after, the Victor McLaglen Motorcycle

Corps performed some "light stunts"; next, the Glendale American Legion Drum and Bugle Corps marched and performed; and then the choir of the People's Independent Church of Christ broke into song. This was followed by an appearance of the American Legion Color Guard and another performance of the cycle corps, which featured stunts and trick riding. More bands and festivities continued until Ronald Reagan ascended the stage, stepped to the microphone, and announced he would serve as master of ceremonies for the rest of the night's proceedings. He introduced a number of entertainers, including Eddie Anderson (Rochester on the *Jack Benny Show*). Each gave bravura performances.

At 9:15 PM the assemblage was informed that the national broadcast of the president's address would begin at 9:30 PM. At 9:24 PM Reagan alerted the crowd that the band would now play the "Star Spangled Banner." This was followed by a display of fireworks. The president took his seat at 9:28 PM. A CBS network announcer introduced Truman's radio address as follows: "This broadcast comes from Gilmore Stadium in Los Angeles, California, and here to describe the scene is Mr. Ronald Reagan." Reagan then remarked:

This is Ronald Reagan speaking from the Gilmore Stadium in Los Angeles, California, where tonight some 30,000 people have packed this stadium waiting to listen to our great President, Harry S. Truman. Loud speakers and television are carrying the meeting to additional thousands on the outside who lost out in the scramble for seats. In a city famous for its spectacles, this is the greatest ever staged for a political rally. Overhead, multicolored searchlights are turning the night sky into a gigantic rainbow. We have just concluded a tremendous program with ten bands, choruses, color guards, motion picture stars, and everything. It has been a great day for President Truman. And this is a fitting climax. Cheering hundreds of thousands jammed the streets of Los Angeles a few hours ago as he drove from the train to his hotel. This is typical of the great outpouring of enthusiasm the President has been receiving all through California.

Reagan then introduced the Honorable George Luckey, chair of the Southern California Democratic State Committee who, in turn, would introduce the president to those assembled and to the national audience tuned to the radio for the speech.[33]

At 9:30 PM the president approached the flag-draped podium and stepped sprightly up to the microphones to begin his address. Packaged in red, white, and blue and meant to deliver a blow to all those who had questioned his domestic policy and his international leadership, Truman began his address with a familiar analogy meant to establish his personal ethos. "This is a championship fight. And I am convinced of one thing: the American people are sold on the idea that nobody deserves to win a championship fight by running away. I do not believe that anybody is going to win this fight by running away from the record or ducking the issues." He next articulated a set of polarized values that helped him frame the differences between the Democrats and the Republicans. His was a classic populist appeal wrapped in the rhetorical defense of New Deal principles: "The underlying struggle in this campaign is a struggle between two sets of ideals. The Democratic ideal of America is summed up in the Four Freedoms: Freedom from Want; Freedom from Fear; Freedom of Worship; and Freedom of Speech. The Republican ideal, as I have seen it in action, is summed up in one phrase, 'Big business first.'"

Truman, who never mentioned his opponent Thomas E. Dewey by name, associated the Republicans with those "shrewd men" who "aim to take advantage of the prosperity which you have attained in the last few years." The audience knew the president was referring to Dewey when he accused the Republicans of "trying their best to avoid any suggestion that there is something to fight about in this campaign. They are trying to lull you to sleep with 'high-level' platitudes. They are saying in effect: 'Everything is all right, everything will go on being all right, if you will just forget about politics and leave things to us.'" Truman issued a ringing denial of that kind of thinking: "But that is not true. . . . These past 2 years have shown us evidence—frightening evidence—that if the country falls into the hands of the leaders of the Republican Party, everything is likely to be all wrong within a very short time." Once again, the president argued forcefully that the wellspring of the people's prosperity had been achieved under Democratic leadership. Truman concretely and explicitly spelled out the coalition he was trying to build and argued forcefully that the Democrats had been central to the well-being of each of the groups he singled out: "Farmers, workers, homeowners, small businessmen—every American has reason to remember the constructive work of the Democratic administrations since 1933: social security; the farm program; collective bargaining; the minimum wage law; slum clearance; low-rent housing; TVA; soil conservation; reclamation and irrigation projects; full employment; world leadership; the highest standards of living in the history of the world. You can sum up in these few words an era of progress with Democratic administrations which believed in the people and worked for the people." The president employed facts and figures as tropes for speaking directly, honestly, and in a forthright fashion. This served a dual purpose—educating the voters on his particular positions as well as a means of contrasting his straightforward, no-nonsense approach to the "shrewd men" who led the opposition. He also used the opportunity to sound off on the specific issues that were important to the constituents he needed to unify for a victory in November. Thus, the president advanced detailed discussions on housing, health care, and inflation, among others. He relied on a description of the local situation as a prelude to a description of his own national efforts, which had been stymied by his Republican opponents. Time and again, on almost every significant domestic issue, Truman would associate the Republicans with some special interest group or lobby that undermined the interests of the people. This offensive barrage provided the bulk of his attack, but when necessary he defended himself well.

The housing shortage was attributed to the "million dollar real estate lobby," which conspired with the House of Representatives to kill the Wagner-Ellender-Taft housing bill—"a long range program to provide 15 million new homes"—using unparalleled "trickery." Truman fashioned a graphic discourse intended to portray his opponents as heartless, cold-blooded folk who think nothing of inflicting needless pain. The housing issue also allowed the president to reinforce his theme of a "do-nothing" Congress, harkening back to the failed legislation of the special session: "Last July, because the need for housing was so desperate, I called a special session of the 80th Congress. Since the Republican National Convention had specifically endorsed slum-clearance and low-rental housing in its platform, I hoped that we could finally get some action. But the real-estate lobby was still at work, and again the Republican Congress obeyed the voice of its masters. The House Republicans blocked the bill." By highlighting the Republican's inability to uphold their own platform's stated goals, Truman emphasized how integral and inimical special interests were in his opponents' political calculations.

Blame for the paucity of decent health care is attributed to the medical lobbies and Congress: "We worked out a painstaking plan for national medical care. It was designed to meet the medical needs of the American people. It provided for new hospitals, clinics, health centers, research, and a system of national health insurance. Who opposed it? The well-organized medical lobby. Who killed it? The Republican 80th 'do-nothing' Congress." Linking lobbies to Republicans and Republicans to lobbies and special interests was a rhetorical strategy that had resonance for those who were having a hard time with such basics as housing and health care. It was a mantra that was repetitive but also effective.

Finally, Truman defended himself against charges of political posturing on the high cost of living, and he employed a familiar scapegoat:

The story of the fight on inflation is especially revealing. When I called the Congress into special session this summer, I urged it to deal with the high cost of living. The Republican leadership replied that this was a political maneuver on my part in an election year.

Let's nail that one right now. The Republicans know perfectly well that I had previously called a special session of the . . . Congress in November 1947 to deal with inflation and the high cost of living. And 1947 was not an election year.

When I called the special session for the same purpose in 1948, it was because the Congress had failed to act for the preceding year and a half.

The dangers of inflation are continuing to grow. The cost of living is continuing to rise. The Republicans cannot conceal their responsibility by hurling charges of "politics" at me.

Laborers, whether on farms, in industries, or supporting small businesses, usually suffer disproportionately from a lack of sustained and effective programs addressing problems like housing, health care, and periodic periods of inflation. These are the constituents Truman champions. Truman's rhetoric underscored vintage New Deal and Fair Deal Democratic politics.

Truman characterized his election bid as a "decisive battle in the life of our country" and a "struggle between the forward forces of liberalism and the backward forces of reaction." The president was not merely making either/or arguments; he was offering potential voters a clear choice and making that choice seem as inevitable as common sense. In arguing that the voters' self-interests were part and parcel of the national interest that could only be accomplished under a Democratic administration, Truman mounted a narrative of inevitability spiced with a little invective and a good measure of common sense.

Truman turned next to his planned discussion of international affairs. Confronting domestic fears of war and Henry Wallace's third-party challenge directly, the president acknowledged, "There are . . . some people with true liberal convictions, whose worry over the state of the world has caused them to lean toward a third party. To these liberals I would say in all sincerity: Think again." Truman argued that Wallace's party did not represent true American ideals. He premised this appeal on two main arguments: (1) "Communists are guiding and using the third party" and (2) "[I]t is folly for any liberal to put his hope in this third party" because "it has no power in the Government and no chance of achieving power" and therefore "cannot achieve peace." Only the "Democratic Party is the party which truly expresses the hopes of American liberals, and which has power to fulfill those hopes. We have worked for peace in a difficult international situation, and we shall continue with all our strength to work for peace." Thus, Truman accused the Wallaceites of being overly influenced by the communists and unable to sustain enough votes to influence the election. To reinforce his major claims, Truman issues a series of specific arguments against support for the Wallace ticket. He charged that a vote for a third party would "only weaken the efforts of the Democratic Party to build a healthy nation and a peaceful world"; "play . . . into the hands" of reactionary Republicans "whose aims are opposed to the aims of American liberalism"; and actually injure "the cause of American liberalism." His final plea was simple and direct: "Think again. Don't waste your vote." In closing his address Truman made an appeal for unity: "This is the hour for the liberal forces of America to unite. We have hopes to fulfill and goals to attain. Together we can rout the forces of reaction once again. We are strong in faith and strong in energy. We must entrust our destiny to those who will safeguard our rights, our freedom, and our national honor."[34]

In Los Angeles, Truman positioned his candidacy as one that would defend the people, continue to advance progressive policies, uphold traditional liberalism, and, in the process, keep the peace at home and abroad. The president argued that the 1948 election represented a national referendum on who could best accomplish this vital task. He left his audiences with a clear mandate: by endorsing him in the upcoming election, they were also helping America win a "decisive battle." As portrayed in these presidential appeals, the election transcends the candidate and the individual voter. A vote, dutifully cast, was much more than a mere vote; it was depicted rhetorically as a ritual of national renewal, one that could restore a proper liberalism and rekindle national ideals. The argument also allowed Truman to embody and sustain rising national expectations.

Upon completing his address, the president left the speaking stand as the band struck up "The Missouri Waltz." Reagan returned to the CBS microphone and described the twenty-one-gun salute that accompanied the president's convoy as it circled around the track of Gilmore Stadium. As the president made his final farewell, the band played "Stars and Stripes Forever." At 9:58 PM, Reagan turned the microphone back to the CBS announcer.[35] The event, tightly scripted, had gone off in a precise, well-executed fashion. Truman had delivered "one of his best

campaign speeches."[36] The president left beaming, flashing a wide grin
as his motorcar left the stadium and sped up to get back to the train
and back on schedule.

Along with major speeches that covered distinct national topics that
the president wanted to air as pivotal to his campaign and the interests
of his constituents, it became clear that on this transcontinental tour
the rear-platform remarks were taking on a distinct form and substance
of their own. As Mutual Broadcasting correspondent Charter Heslep
observed, "Truman's platform speeches have developed a set pattern
quickly. After the usual greetings, localized in most instances, he plays
the 'do nothing Congress' theme. Sometimes it gets a good hand. Then
come the local references. This is followed by a sort of 'you got what you
deserved' act as he chides them for not voting in 1946. Then he plugs
the local candidates and concludes by pointing out that if they elected
the Democrat tickets, he won't have to go house hunting because his
name is at the top of that ticket."[37]

A rear-platform address typical of the western tour and representative of Heslep's identification of an emerging pattern is perhaps best
encountered in Truman's whistle-stop remarks in Colton, California,
on September 24, 1948. Delivered the day after the major speech in Los
Angeles at Gilmore Stadium, the following analysis reveals the generic
elements in Truman's rhetorical method and simultaneously demonstrates how he adapted his message to his audiences at each train stop.
Typically, the president's whistle-stop remarks would unfold in four
distinct phases.

First, Truman would greet the crowd, thank the people for turning
out, and indicate that similar crowds had been turning out to see him
all along his train route, an indication of the enthusiasm and interest
in his campaign. The president always would begin with an opening
greeting:

> I certainly do appreciate this most cordial welcome to Colton.
> It's wonderful. I don't see where all the people came from. In San
> Diego this morning at 8:30 by standard time, 9:30 California time,
> there were 25,000 people out in the ball park and there must have

been 50,000 on the street besides that. I never saw anything like that crowd that early in the morning. That's been the sort of reception we have been receiving all over the State, so I know you're interested. I know you're interested in how the President stands and what he stands for, and in words of one syllable, I've been telling the people of California just where I stand, and I think they understand that.

Second, he issued a wake-up call to warn the voters of Republican intent, arguing that Republican philosophies and goals were decidedly inimical to the interests of the people:

Now, we're up against this same thing all across the board in this campaign. I explained to the farmers in Iowa and to the whole Nation that their interests are being jeopardized by the policies of the Republican Congress, and that's only a sample of what they can expect to get if the Republicans get complete control of the Congress.

Republicans are just simply tools of big business. [The Democrats, on the other hand, are different:] We believe that there ought to be a fair distribution of the wealth so that the farmer gets a part of the income, the laboring man gets his part, the small businessman gets his part, and then the distribution is as it should be.

The basic issue in this campaign is as simple as can be: it's the special interests against the people; the special interests against the people. And that was conclusively proved by the Republican "do nothing" Congress which we just finished with—thank God.

Truman consistently argued that in abandoning the Democratic ticket voters could full well expect the Republicans to "tear them apart."

Third, Truman argued that Republican control of Congress had led to deleterious effects for the region. He often stressed local or state issues of import to those assembled: "You know what they did to your irrigation and reclamation and water projects in this great State. They would have sabotaged every single one of them if it hadn't been for such fellows as this [a reference to Democratic Congressmen Sheppard] and for the President of the United States. I can say that conclusively, and he'll back up every word I say."

Fourth, at the close of his remarks, Truman would make an appeal for the vote, often asking the locals to vote for all the candidates on the Democratic ticket. Time and again, he would ask his listeners to vote for their own self-interest, and time and again that self-interest was described as best represented in and advanced by the Democratic Party: "Now, I want you to use good judgment. I want you to use good judgment, and I'm sure you will. You go to the polls on November 2nd and take no chances. Just vote the Democratic ticket straight, and then you won't have anything to worry about—we'll have a Democratic Congress and a Democratic President. And I won't be troubled by this terrible housing shortage, for I can stay in the White House for another 4 years."[38] Good judgment translated into protecting one's self-interests, and that was only accomplished by voting for the president and his party. It was simple, it was direct, it was delivered with a touch of humor, and it came to have powerful resonance with the voters who had sometimes waited hours to catch a glimpse of history at the small depots or in loose-knit assemblies along some desolate area where the tracks and the fate of scheduling made the president available for a brief train stop.

At this and countless other whistle-stops, Truman spoke bluntly and directly to his key constituencies: farmers, laborers, and small business owners. He warned time and again that the present prosperity enjoyed by these sectors under Democratic leadership would be jeopardized with the Republicans in control: "The farmers got the greatest income they ever had. Labor got the greatest income they ever had, and business has done better than it's ever done in the history of the country. Now, why do you want to throw that out the window? You have a good chance to do it, if you don't go to the polls and vote and let these birds know where you stand."[39] Truman's metaphors were homely, but direct, and custom-tailored to the kind of down-home reasoning any common citizen could respect: Why would someone want to throw prosperity "out the window"? Truman hoped those assembled would conclude resoundingly: "My vote ought to mean something; the least I can do is show 'these birds' where I stand!"

For the most part, Truman pressed the case on domestic issues in two primary ways: First, he blamed Republicans for present problems. Second, he predicted future ones if they were given a chance to continue present practices. In general, this format was employed time and again in the rear-platform remarks. The repetition might have worn down reporters on the train, but each speech at each stop was new to the denizens of the particular city, town, or hamlet where the train paused to introduce its famous rider. Truman seemed positively energized at each stop and showed few signs of fatigue. His enthusiasm never waned. He seemed to almost welcome the rigors of the long, repetitive days on the campaign trail. It was clear that the crowds energized him, and he returned the favor gladly. As Karabell concluded, "[W]hat was most important of all was how Truman touched people and how they responded."[40]

Upon his return from the western trip, a reporter asked the president how he was holding up physically. Truman answered sprightly, "I could start right up tomorrow and do it all over again and take you all with me." The assembled press corps heaved a deep communal groan at this response. One reporter playfully asked about Truman's "despicable" routine of rising at five o'clock each morning. "Truman grinned and replied: 'Well, yes, it's hard work, but I like to work because it's in a good cause.'"[41]

At Union Station in Washington, D.C., Truman, "nattily dressed and apparently unwearied," delivered a short recap of his western trip. He was met by about fifteen hundred people. Included among them were "pretty girls carrying such placards as 'You won the first round—keep punching,' and 'Don't make a move unless it's For Truman.'" Before his brief talk, he was greeted with a rousing rendition of "Hail to the Chief," which was played by the Metropolitan Police Boys Club Band. After the brief talk, clusters of people gathered on the street corners to watch as Truman's planned motorcade made its way back to the White House; this served as a final symbol of what was thought to have been a helpful, if not triumphant, leg of the campaign tour. The total number of people who witnessed Truman's return to the White House was estimated at fifty to seventy-five thousand.[42] Meanwhile, "political analysts and polls continued to report a decided trend in favor of Governor Dewey, [while] the White House and Democratic headquarters claimed that President Truman had gained much from the two-week transcontinental trip."[43]

The western leg of the train tour had precipitated an enlivened public discussion of the issues in the 1948 campaign. As one report noted, by the end of the western tour, "There [wa]s a conviction among many on the Truman train, including those who don't give the President any chance of winning this year, that sooner or later Governor Dewey is going to have to abandon his 'campaign of cliches' and get more specific about his program or risk the loss of votes from people who, while never enthusiastic about Mr. Truman and longing for a change, still aren't ready to 'buy a pig in a poke.'"[44] Truman's unique combination of political needling and friendly banter was at least entertaining. His energetic and consistent take on the issues also was beginning to make sense. His opponent's voice was raised in glittering generalities that while filled with a kind of erudition, if not eloquence, began to pale in comparison with the president's unpolished but nevertheless sincere Everyman persona.

————◆◆◆————

The Fall Campaign Continues, October–November 1948

After a brief hiatus in early October, Truman set out again on a three-day train tour October 6 through 8. He visited Delaware, Pennsylvania, New Jersey, and New York. This trip included major speeches in Philadelphia on October 6 and Buffalo on October 8. Three days later, the president would attack the Midwest with an October 11 through 16 itinerary that would take him through the heartland with stops in Ohio, Indiana, Illinois, Wisconsin, Minnesota, and finally, looping back to West Virginia. Major speeches on this segment of the train tour were delivered in Akron, Springfield, St. Paul, Madison, Milwaukee, and Indianapolis.

On October 18 and 19 Truman traveled by airplane to Florida and North Carolina for major campaign speeches in Miami and Raleigh. On October 23 Truman once again boarded the train for a tour through Pennsylvania with major speeches in Scranton, Wilkes-Barre, Johnstown, and Pittsburgh. The final train tour of the campaign would begin with stops in Indiana, Illinois, Ohio, Massachusetts, Connecticut, Rhode Island, and New York from October 25 to October 30. Stops included major addresses in Gary, Chicago, Cleveland, Boston, New York, Harlem, and Brooklyn. Then Truman would head west again with stops scheduled in Ohio, Indiana, Illinois, and Missouri. On October

30, he delivered a final major address in St. Louis. On Nov 1, election eve, Truman went to Kansas City and, finally, motored to record his vote on November 2 in his hometown, officially ending the campaign in Independence, Missouri, where he delivered election-eve remarks to a national radio audience.[1]

The midwestern leg of the tour helped establish Truman's credentials with the heartland. A more extended discussion of this leg of the tour will facilitate a better understanding of the president's attempts at persuading key constituents. Despite a grueling speaking schedule with multiple daily stops, the candidate consistently maintained a positive attitude. Prior to boarding the train for the Midwest, Truman was asked how he felt. "Perfect," he replied, flashing a wide grin.[2]

In preparing for a particular stop, aides typically developed an itinerary for the president that included a listing of the time of arrival, time of departure, means of arrival (train line and/or necessary motorcade), name of the local chairperson in charge, the specific location of the president's appearance, security arrangements, a list of persons boarding the train, another list describing who would appear on the platform with the president and the requisite introductions, a brief outline of speech material, a listing of dignitaries and people the president should be familiar with in the particular city or town, and finally, any pertinent notes speechwriters deemed helpful.

For example, the speech material for the Richmond, Indiana, stopover on October 12 included a description of Richmond (e.g., it was an industrial town, a center for Quaker culture, and the home of Earlham College), its population (35,174 in 1940), and news that it was a "Republican stronghold" that last voted for the Democratic ticket in 1932 and 1936. After listing various dignitaries, the itinerary included a last brief note: "President Truman will be presented with a bouquet of 'Hill's Better Time Roses' developed during the Depression. The Hill Company is 100% Republican, and some comment could be made concerning these 'Better Time Roses.'"[3]

As noted previously, while he never delivered exactly the same speech twice, Truman's fall campaign whistle-stop rear-platform remarks had by now developed a common organizational pattern, but each was adapted to the particular town, locality, or region. Where possible, Truman also used the rear-platform speeches to promote his major speeches, which were often scheduled later in the day or in the evening. If the major speech of the day had already been delivered, he would say, "I hope you had the chance to hear my speech" in Akron or Milwaukee or wherever he happened to dispense with a major message in the vicinity of a particular whistle-stop.

The trip to the Midwest was a particular challenge. As one pundit noted, "He is heading into the heart of 'enemy territory,' although most of these states were in the Democratic column four years ago."[4] As Truman barnstormed the nation's farm country, he had to convince prosperous farmers that they had a stake in the election. As Charter Heslep wrote to his wife while traveling with the president on the train, "We are passing thru a lot of excellent Ohio farm country and it all looks prosperous. Prosperity is one of Truman's handicaps. People aren't impressed with cries of what may happen if their stomachs are full."[5] Truman was determined to convince the heartland that prosperity was an uncertain commodity, especially if guardianship was handed to the Republicans.

A focus on particular segments during a two-day period of the midwestern tour as the president's train traversed Ohio and Illinois should yield additional insight as to the flavor of Truman's appeals and demonstrate how he tirelessly tried to meet the heavy challenge. On October 11, 1948, Truman delivered eleven speeches at eleven different locations in Ohio. These included prepared remarks for a breakfast in Cincinnati, which required a speech at 8:35 AM, rear-platform remarks in Hamilton, Ohio, at 10:17 AM, a formal address in Dayton at 11:50 AM, followed by a series of other whistle-stop rear-platform remarks as the campaign train made its way across Ohio. After stopping at a final whistle-stop in Rittman Ohio at 6:30 PM, the president had delivered ten speeches either as formal addresses or in back-platform remarks.[6] Then Truman proceeded to Akron to deliver a major address on labor at nine o'clock that evening.[7]

The major addresses at Cincinnati and Dayton provide worthy exemplars of Truman's attempts to identify with the locals and extend his credentials as a legitimate public servant. At Cincinnati, at the Netherlands Plaza Hotel, Truman delivered a formal breakfast address. Approximately twelve hundred people attended at two dollars a plate. In typical Truman style, the president drew upon old memories to establish his identification with the region and to make his audience feel comfortable: "I think it was in 1930, I paid a visit to Hamilton County, Ohio, because you had an assessment system here that seemed to me to be a just one. I tried to get that system implemented in Jackson County, Mo., when I was head of government there in Jackson, but I didn't have any luck; but I still think you have a great assessment system. I don't know whether it is still in effect or not, but it seemed to be the most just one in the country."

As he would do in many of his whistle-stop remarks, at the end of this address Truman would gain added credibility as a crowd-pleaser by introducing his family. He said, "Now I usually take my greatest assets around the country with me. How would you like to meet my family? I will present Mrs. Truman first—she runs me and the White House. Now I have the privilege of presenting my baby, my daughter, Margaret." This homespun bantering always seemed to be appreciated. Sometimes, however, Bess complained a bit when the president would introduce her as "the Boss." One eyewitness reported Margaret was actually "furious" when the president introduced her to "the big breakfast crowd" at Cincinnati as "'my baby.'"[8] But audiences loved it. Truman continued these rehearsed but nonetheless heartfelt introductions throughout the campaign.

At Dayton's Memorial Hall, in a formal address, Truman continued his identification with Ohio voters and simultaneously stressed his public service record: "I am acquainted with this great city of yours. Years and years ago, long before we had paved roads in the United States, Dayton was a center of road boosters. Since I was a road booster, and still am, I used to come to Dayton and discuss with the people here in this city the necessity for a transcontinental paved highway from Baltimore to Los Angeles. We have this highway now, and we are going to get a good lot of other things too."

In this speech, he focused on three major issues: "peace, prices, and places to live." One suspects that the president hoped the alliterative ring would help people remember his remarks and his platform. Truman also promoted an address to be broadcast from Akron later that evening: "I hope you will listen to my broadcast tonight in Akron. I am going to take the hide off 'em [i.e., the Eightieth Congress] from top to bottom. I hate to have to do that, but they have it coming. Just listen to the speech. When I get through with that . . . speech, they won't have any hide left." The president's colloquialisms seemed to play well in Ohio, but things said in the heat of the campaign can sometimes go awry. As Heslep noted, "At Dayton, Truman almost made a bad slip. I thought I might be seeing something, but at least half a dozen others got exactly the same expression. We had gotten a terrific ovation when he said he was going to 'take the hide off 'em from top to bottom.' Apparently, carried away by the enthusiasm, he almost lost control of himself. He said, 'when I get thru [with] that . . . ' and here we heard a feint 'g' sound and instantly his tongue came to his lips and what all of us thought was that he cut off the cuss word 'goddam.'"[9]

As Truman traveled across Ohio, he demonstrated his knowledge of the local areas. At 4:05 PM the train stopped in Fostoria. Here Truman attacked the Republican's chief campaign theme—"unity":

> Dwight and Andrew tell me that Fostoria used to be two towns. In 1854 they united and became the prosperous community of Fostoria. Unity has helped you people here build a strong community, the kind of community that some of these Ohio Republicans call, 'whistle-stops.' Well, I say thank God for the whistle-stops of our country. They are the backbone of the Nation. They have got the people who produce the Nation's goods and the Nation's food—and they have got the people who are going to keep the Democratic administration in the White House and elect a Democratic House and a Democratic Senate in the coming election. The kind of unity that built Fostoria is something that I can go for. It is the kind of unity that helped build this Nation. It's the kind of unity that helped win the war. I can understand that and I like it. That's why I had that kind of unity in this administration. But I'll tell you frankly, I don't understand the phony unity that the Republican candidates are talking about.

Truman directly confronted his entrance into enemy territory: "They tell me that Seneca County is a Republican county. Well, that's all right with me. I want the Republicans of Seneca County to know what I think—and I think if they have open minds, they will vote in their interests, just the same as the Democrats will, and that will be to vote the Democratic ticket." In what had now become a trademark in his back-platform speeches, Truman gently scolded his listeners for their lack of participation in the midterm elections: "You know, in 1946 a third of the people elected the 80th Congress. Two-thirds of you stayed at home. And look what you got! You got just what you deserved. You got a good kicking around, just as soon as they had an opportunity to give it to you. Now, if you do that again, you won't have anybody to blame but yourselves."

Truman offered his audiences nothing earth-shatteringly new, nothing in any sense profound, just straight talk on the bread-and-butter issues; just a simple, often dire warning about the stakes involved in the 1948 election, and, in the process, he conveyed a sincerity that seemed to win the people's confidence. When Truman spoke one got the sense that he knew what he was talking about, that his interests very much overlapped with those of his audience because he acted and sounded like one of the regulars, a neighbor, or trusted friend. At times, he posed as a wise old physician with a prescription for what ailed the populace and presumed to draw an easy-going medicine from his political medicine bag. Both the doctor who dispensed the prescription and the patients who took it did so in a relationship of mutual earned trust.

Truman's back-platform speech in Willard, Ohio, delivered less than an hour after the stop in Fostoria, was identified by David McCullough as "a perfect example of Truman the barnstormer at top form."[10] McCullough was so impressed he published the entire speech in his Truman biography.[11] It is not clear that Willard was the occasion for Truman's best whistle-stop speech, but it is clear that he arrived with a vibrant and pointed message. In Willard, Truman proclaimed confidently: "There is not a single, solitary man or woman in the United States today who can't find out in two minutes where I stand on the important matters like foreign policy, labor, agriculture, social security, housing, high prices, and all the other problems we as a nation have to face. But there is not a single, solitary man or woman in the United States who has been able, within the last 2 months, to find out where the Republican candidate stands on these issues." Not only did Truman chide the Republicans for ducking the issues, he made sure the voters knew that a vote cast for Truman would be well spent: Vote "your own interests," Truman told the crowd, "and when you vote in your own interests . . . you cannot do anything else but vote the straight Democratic ticket." Wherever the president went, he was well-received. Over time, the crowds began to grow, and the campaign picked up speed as Truman pounded home his agenda and received little by way of refutation from his opponent.

The next day, October 12, Truman delivered a back-platform speech in Decatur, Illinois, that both typified his approach to the Midwest and underlined his resolve to continue to take his fight for the presidency directly to the people by touching upon issues of immediate concern to constituents in the regions he visited. At Decatur, Truman most clearly revealed his populist strategy for convincing farmers, laborers, and small businessmen that their interests were at stake. The entire text of this speech appears preceding this book's introduction, so it will not be repeated here.

Analysis of Truman's Decatur back-platform remarks reveals an excellent example of Truman's whistle-stop strategies. He acknowledges his appreciation for the turnout. By revealing his method for estimating the crowds, he adds a common touch. The president contrasted twelve years of "Republican misrule" that led to the Depression with those of the Roosevelt era, touting a record of performance that led labor to its "fair share," farmers to "parity," and small business to a "square deal."

"Since we are enjoying our present great prosperity," Truman argued, "why can't it just continue on like this?" He answers his own question: "We can't count on continued prosperity going on just like this because we have so many serious problems that need action, and they need action now." Republicans had refused to confront and act on the crucial issues. Truman argued that the "80th do-nothing Congress" was "trying to pretend that there aren't any issues." By blocking the "truth," the "reactionary Republicans, completely under the thumb of the lobbies of the special interests," subverted the national interest. This populist appeal certainly positioned the president as an anti-elitist representative of the people. Just as important, Truman's recitation of Republican indifference and inaction was supported by concrete examples, each of which had potential for arousing fears, even among the prosperous.

Whether it was reducing high prices, defending the rights of labor, ensuring enough housing, supplying hydroelectric power, guaranteeing farm price supports, or providing rural electrification and conservation, Truman protested that his hands had been tied at every turn, and as a result, "the Republican 80th Congress, which the Republican candidate for President has warmly endorsed, undermined the very foundation of the prosperity of the American people as they are enjoying it now."

Truman reasoned that farmers, laborers, and businesspersons had common cause because the success of each was interdependent. After all, "When the farmers and the workers are well off, then the businessmen are able to do well." Having established his premise by fact and reasoning, the president, in typical back-platform style would encourage his audience: "Vote for yourselves; vote in your own interest." A vote on behalf of self-interest was always depicted as a simultaneous vote for the national interest. In concluding his remarks, Truman reinforced his signature populist appeal: "I hope that you will make the right choice and that you'll have a government that has the interests of the people at heart, a government headed by Democrats—who believe in Democratic principles, who believe in the welfare of the whole country, and not just in the welfare of a special few." Truman's direct style isolated upon both the enemy and the issues, and he hammered on each throughout the campaign. He seemed to believe in what he said and what he said was gaining the attention and the allegiance of the coalition of voters he sought to patch together.

In the latter part of October, as the campaign approached its denouement, Truman returned to Pennsylvania, stopping in cities such as Wilkes-Barre, Scranton, Johnstown, and Pittsburgh. The president's visit to Pittsburgh is memorable for an especially creative attack on

Dewey. It began with an eight-mile torchlight parade. Along the way people stood from five to twenty deep. Truman addressed a crowd of fifteen thousand at the Hunt Armory. Here Truman demonstrated he could not only joke with his audience but also that he was not above a theatrical twist or two. In tauntingly tongue-in-cheek fashion, Mr. Truman, with the able assistance of speechwriter David Lloyd, concocted a now-famous imaginary dialogue between the American people, cast as patient, and his unnamed opponent, cast as, in Truman's words, "a kind of doctor with a magic cure for all mankind." The script went as follows:

> Doctor: "You have been bothered much by issues lately?"
> Patient: "Not bothered, exactly. Of course we've had quite a few …"
> Doctor: *(tugging an imaginary mustache):* "You shouldn't think about issues. What you need is my brand of soothing syrup—I call it 'unity.'"
> Patient: "What is wrong with me?"
> Doctor: "I never discuss issues with a patient. But what you need is a major operation. Not very serious. It will just mean taking out the complete works and putting in a Republican administration."

This scripted imaginary dialogue was a direct attack against a hapless Dewey and an overwhelming hit with the audience; it was met with shouts, whistles, and howling laughter. The president derisively concluded his narrative by charging: "This soft talk and double talk, this combination of crafty silence and resounding misrepresentation, is an insult to the intelligence of the American public."[12] One news report at the time provided a partisan's-eye-view of Truman's enthusiastic reception in Pittsburgh: "Despite the fact that there were 2.84 million registered Republicans and only 1.8 million Democrats, one plucky Pennsylvania Democratic leader, viewing the audience for the Truman persuasions, would confidently pronounce, 'When they fill even the doorways, windows, and rooftops, it could mean victory.'"[13]

As Truman prepared for his final train tour, one constituency of note—African Americans—had not yet received the president's undivided attention, at least by way of campaign address. Although key to the outcome of the election, Truman actually spoke very little about civil rights during the campaign because "he wanted to avoid further southern defections, rely on the record, and allow lesser candidates to rally the black vote."[14]

Nevertheless, the president was cognizant of the importance of this constituency. He accepted an invitation issued by the Interdenominational Ministers Alliance, a greater New York committee of Protestant African American clergy, which planned to honor him with the Franklin D. Roosevelt Memorial Brotherhood Medal. Truman went to Harlem to accept the award on October 29. The date chosen for the event was anything but haphazard. Exactly one year earlier to the day, on October 29, 1947, Truman's civil rights committee had issued its groundbreaking report. The president used the occasion to commemorate the committee's work and by proxy his own.

After thanking the ministers for the award, Truman referred to the entire night's proceedings as "a most solemn occasion." Not only was the award named after a "great champion of human rights," but it was also meaningful for the hope that the night represented for the nation: "Eventually, we are going to have an America in which freedom and opportunity are the same for everyone. There is only one way to accomplish that great purpose, and that is to keep working for it and never take a backward step." The president praised his committee's report, *To Secure These Rights,* as one written by men and women of "honesty" and "courage." This "momentous" report, the president explained, was also a product of his personal concern: "I created the Civil Rights Committee because racial and religious intolerance began to appear after World War II. They threatened the very freedoms we had fought to save." Truman added, "We Americans have a democratic way of acting when our freedoms are threatened." Michael Gardner argues that the use of the term "we" in this context is important: "By choosing inclusive words like 'we' before his Harlem audience, Truman demonstrated his empathy and his personal appreciation for the fact that all Americans—black and white—had recently joined together and sacrificed collectively and mightily in World War II; and because of that joint sacrifice, Truman let his audience feel his personal repulsion about recent and increasing outbreaks of racial intolerance that had victimized returning black veterans."[15]

By inaugurating the committee and employing this ceremonial occasion to eulogize its work, Truman was provided a unique opportunity to bask in the limelight of his own actions on behalf of civil rights and indeed all of the good the report had accomplished in the year since its release. In reinforcing the solemnity of the occasion, Truman championed the civil rights report as one drawn up "in the tradition of" the key documents fashioned by the Founding Fathers. His rationale was simple but profound. The Declaration of Independence acknowledged "all men are created equal," and the Constitution ensured that "all citizens are equal before the law," and therefore the federal government "has a duty to guarantee to every citizen equal protection of the laws." Moreover, Truman praised his civil rights committee for doing more than merely reminding the nation of its basic creeds: "It described a method to put these principles into action, and to make them a living reality for every American, regardless of his race, his religion, or his national origin." At every level—local, state and national—Truman declared, the committee's work was described as crucial in helping people to realize that when American rights and opportunities were "fully protected and respected . . . then we will have the kind of unity that really means something." In a light but penetrating jab at his Republican opponent, the president expanded on the point: "It is easy to talk of unity. But it is the work that is done for unity that really counts." In a series of parallel statements, the president forcefully reinforced his dream for race relations in America:

The Civil Rights Committee described the kind of freedom that comes when every man has an equal chance for a job—not just the hot and heavy job—but the best job he is qualified for.

The Committee described the kind of freedom that comes when every American boy and girl has an equal chance for an education.

The Committee described the kind of freedom that comes when every citizen has an equal opportunity to go to the ballot box and cast his vote and have it counted.

The Committee described the kind of freedom that comes when every man, woman, and child is free from the fear of mob violence and intimidation.

Progress in these areas also alluded to a cold war imperative: "When we have that kind of freedom, we will face the evil forces that are abroad in the world—whatever or wherever they may be—with the strength that comes from complete confidence in one another and from complete faith in the working of our own democracy." What was accomplished at home strengthened our hand abroad by solidifying our internal relations and making our form of government attractive to others. "One of the great things that the Civil Rights Committee did for the country," the president said, "was to get every American to think seriously about the principles that make our country great." After commending the committee for opening this national dialogue, Truman stressed the far-reaching effects of the committee's efforts and praised its comprehensive approach to solutions in its recommendations. He expressed his hope that the report would continue to be "studied widely."

Truman then linked his civil rights legislation to his executive actions. He was matter of fact but abundantly transparent about where to place blame for the lack of progress on the legislation: "After the Civil Rights Committee submitted its report, I asked Congress to do ten of the things recommended by the Committee. You know what they did about that. So I went ahead and did what the President can do, unaided by the Congress. I issued two Executive orders." Truman also commended the Justice Department's recent argument to the Supreme Court on removing restrictive covenants.

In concluding his address, Truman summarized his work on behalf of civil rights as part of a larger, principled liberal vision. Here again, the shadow of the cold war suffused the words and helped impel an additional sense of the need for united action: "Today the democratic way of life is being challenged all over the world. Democracy's answer to the challenge of totalitarianism is its promise of equal rights and equal opportunity for all mankind. The fulfillment of this promise is among the highest purposes of government. Our determination to attain the goal of equal rights and equal opportunity must be resolute and unwavering." In closing, the president issued a final pledge: "For my part, I intend to keep moving toward this goal with every ounce of strength and determination that I have."[16] This speech, neither lengthy nor necessarily packed with specifics, did provide a "momentous" occasion. The president's final pledge seemed not only heartfelt but ironclad. As Gardner notes, "For the people gathered in Dorrance Brooks Square that day, and for the larger audience of black Americans that read the next day's newspaper accounts of this presidential foray into Harlem, President Truman's words of empathy and determination to reform civil rights in the United States were electrifying."[17]

Harry Truman was addressing a largely black audience, but his message also was directed to the entire county. By invoking the need for equality and recognizing the stakes for the emerging cold war, Truman hoped to appeal to all Americans—piquing their sense of justice and fair play and reminding them of their personal and communal stake in the survival of democracy. So while the Harlem address served as a message of hope in the African American community, it also challenged all Americans to be better and to do better. In the context of the campaign, the Harlem address was a towering recommitment to principles of justice, equality, and opportunity; it provided ringing assurance that the president would continue to press for civil rights.

The next day Truman delivered his final major address of the campaign. Murphy remembers this occasion as something special: "On Saturday afternoon as we were going into St. Louis, the president sat by himself and made notes in his notebook for an hour or more I suppose. When he finally delivered this speech, he didn't look at the draft that had been prepared for him and he didn't look at his own notes. It was, I suppose, the best political speech that he ever made in that campaign or any other time, and it was tremendously exciting and set the crowd wild. He made no use at all of either draft that had been prepared for him; as I say, he didn't look at his own notes; I'm sure he knew what they were. This was one occasion when it certainly was a fine thing for him to depart from and not use the draft."[18]

Kiel Auditorium in St. Louis was filled to capacity. An animated and relaxed president focused on the themes and issues that had been most productive throughout his campaign tour. Truman's energy was at an all-time high as he recapitulated for his home-state audience the common threads of an exhaustive populist rhetorical campaign. The president attacked the "saboteurs and character assassins" who "helped elect" that infernal "Republican 'do-nothing' 80th Congress." He reinforced his principal campaign mantra with a rousing delivery that stirred the assembly: "There is just one big issue in this campaign and that's the people against the special interests. The Republicans stand for special interests, and they always have. The Democratic Party, which I now head, stands for the people—and always has stood for the people." Truman continued to curry favor with his key constituencies until the very end:

The Democrats have believed always that the welfare of the whole people should come first, and that means that the farmers, labor, small businessmen, and everybody else in the country should have a fair share of the prosperity that goes around.

We have placed the farmers in the best position they have ever been in the history of the world.

We have placed labor in its best position it has ever been in the history of the world. And we have been against monopoly from the start.

Now, when farmers are prosperous, and when labor gets good wages, business is bound to be good. And that is the reason the national income is higher in this country than it has ever been before in the history of the world.

Truman left nothing to chance. He ignored any and all enthymematic principles. Simple logic told him and he told the farmers that the farmer "who votes the Republican ticket, ought to have his head examined!" He cajoled: "Most laboringmen stayed away from the polls in 1946—and see what they got! They got the Taft-Hartley Act." Getting to the polls to cast one's vote was depicted as an urgent duty and one that would serve the citizenry well, if cast for the Democratic ticket. The president warned: "If you don't vote on November the 2nd, and you send back an 81st Congress under the same leadership that the 80th Congress had, you will be in some fix sure enough—because the Republicans have already said what they are going to do to labor, if they get control of the Government." The threat of dire consequences, delivered in the colloquial phrase "some fix sure enough," was easily understood and provided a reasonable and immediate motive for action.

Since this speech was one of Truman's last opportunities to communicate in the campaign, he took pains to reinforce his image as a fighter. He boldly took advantage of the pollsters and pundits who had confidently predicted his defeat. He led audiences to infer that his underdog status was nothing new. Truman made his never-say-die, cocksure attitude understandable by familiarizing his audience with his weathered political experience. The president suggested that there was little cause for concern: "Now, my friends, I have been all over these United States from one end to another, and when I started out the song was—well, you can't win—the Democrats can't win. Ninety percent of the press is against us, but that didn't discourage me one little bit. You know, I had four campaigns here in the great State of Missouri, and I never had a metropolitan paper for me that whole time. And I licked them every time!" Truman's indefatigable spirit was on full display in his home state of Missouri.

Finally, Truman concluded with a summation that not only provided a rousing conclusion to the address at Kiel Auditorium but also summed up his rhetorical strategy during the entire campaign, "People are waking up that the tide is beginning to roll, and I am here to tell you that if you do your duty as citizens of the greatest Republic the sun has ever shone on, we will have a Government that will be for your interests, that will be for peace in the world, and for the welfare of all the people, and not just a few."[19] Peace and prosperity with Truman and the Democrats. That was the ticket the president wanted everyone to remember on election day.

Truman had delivered a provocative and lively speech and transformed it into something more. Robert H. Ferrell judged that the president "took over a huge audience and turned it into a raging democratic mob."[20] Robert J. Donovan gave the once inept speaker high praise, claiming triumphantly that Truman "had Kiel Auditorium rocking."[21] All of the experimentation with Truman's style of public speaking had finally returned dividends. This "off-the-cuff" address represented the culmination of a viscerally taxing and unimaginably stressful campaign; it was also a ringing confirmation of Truman's newfound rhetorical prowess. Having tested the political waters for so long, having found the formula for extemporaneous address—one that fit the man, highlighted the personality, and found the delicate balance of a personal comfort zone—the president threw out his speech drafts in St. Louis and had at it. It was a bravura performance, but it was one that had been a long time in the making and one that had been decidedly hard won through persistent rehearsal.

Truman spoke like a man on a mission. His populist appeals were tailored to a constituency he knew he could count on. The president argued convincingly that, if elected, he would continue to do his part to address the issues vigorously and convert the campaign promises he made into a better and stronger America. All of this structure of feeling was built into the narrative Truman had improbably created. The style, the delivery, and the sincere conviction all conspired to push forward a viable candidate, mitigating for some, if not erasing for others, what had been an inviolable tenet of the 1948 campaign: the president was a "dead duck." Truman's political resurrection was in large part a matter of words. Words have consequences. The Kiel Auditorium speech was the best evidence presented to date that this candidate was not only alive and well but that the train tour had seasoned and transformed him into something quite unique and formidable.

David McCullough has written that Harry S. Truman "was on a crusade for the welfare of every man."[22] The evidence in Truman's public discourse in prepared campaign addresses and whistle-stop remarks certainly confirms this conclusion. Nevertheless, many had yet to be convinced that the president would ultimately prevail. On October 31, the *New York Times* issued a "Last Minute Forecast" based on its compilation of state survey results predicting electoral college votes. The *Times* count was as follows: Dewey: 345; Truman: 105; Thurmond: 38; Doubtful: 43.[23] Thomas E. Dewey was regarded as a "certain winner." As *Washington Post* reporter Edward T. Folliard noted, "Should it turn out otherwise and Mr. Truman be the winner, the polltakers and the prognosticators would be forced into the greatest crow-eating debauch in the annals of American politics."[24]

On November 1, election eve, the president delivered his final campaign speech in a national radio broadcast originating from Truman's living room in Independence, Missouri. The president concluded with a simple, heartfelt appeal to his fellow citizens: "[T]he future welfare of our country is in your hands. I have told you the truth as God has given me wisdom to see the truth."[25] At 10:00 AM on November 2, 1948, Harry S. Truman, with a full complement of news reporters and photographers in tow, cast the 101st ballot in his home precinct in Independence, Missouri. One reporter asked, "Mr. President, how do you think it is going?" Flashing that trademark wide grin, he replied, "Why, it can't be anything but a victory."[26] When Truman went to bed on the night of November 2, the election results were still being tabulated. He woke up the next morning to learn that his confidence had not been misplaced. Truman had managed to garner 24,179,259 votes (49.6% of the popular vote); Dewey received 21,991,291 votes (45.1% of the popular vote). Truman prevailed in 38 states; Dewey had taken 16. Truman was awarded 303 electoral votes while Dewey managed to secure only 189.[27] It was a stunning victory.

After Truman won the election, he climbed back aboard the *Ferdinand Magellan* and set out from Missouri to travel back to Washington. Along the way, he delivered "victory" speeches in Independence, St. Louis, Vincennes, and Cincinnati. The seventeen-car train then proceeded on to a triumphant return to Washington, D.C.[28] When his train stopped in Vincennes the president greeted those assembled and thanked them for voting "exactly right." Truman shared the emotion of the moment: "I do not feel elated at the victory—I feel overwhelmed with the responsibility. Just bear that in mind. Now, good luck to all of you, and I hope—I sincerely hope—that you will not be disappointed in the result."[29] Such public humility was vintage Truman.

The president was scheduled to return to Union Station at 11:00 AM. He would deliver brief remarks in front of Union Station to those assembled at the Columbus statue and then travel by motorcade southwest on Delaware Avenue to Constitution Avenue where it intersected Pennsylvania Avenue and proceed up Pennsylvania Avenue and ultimately to the White House. Large American flags were draped on the street poles along the motorcade route; the Marine, Army, Air Force, Metropolitan Police Boys, Metropolitan Police, and Washington Redskins bands were all stationed along the route to provide a festive, patriotic musical celebration. At Post Square, firefighters erected six one-hundred-foot ladders to form an archway for welcome signs as additional fire and police personnel patrolled the parade route.[30] When Truman arrived at the White House he exclaimed, "I can't tell you how very much I appreciate this warm and cordial welcome to the Capital City of the greatest Nation on earth. It is overwhelming. It makes a man study and wonder whether he is worthy of the confidence, worthy of the responsibility which has been thrust upon him. I will say this to you, that I expect to work just as hard for you as I have done for you up to date, and to do it to the best of my ability."[31] While the president was humble in victory, many were shocked by this unforeseen outcome, and they vigorously sought an explanation.

Why Truman Won: The Rhetorical Roots of a Homespun Victory

Harry S. Truman achieved "the greatest upset in American political history."[1] The "wiseacres" had been proven dead wrong. Pollsters and pundits sputtered back to their respective offices to try to explain the inexplicable. While opinions differed over the reasons for Truman's upset victory, Truman's own hand was given a prominent place in the mix: "It is evident that Mr. Truman won because he conducted a terrific campaign, carrying the attack to his GOP opponent with a fury not matched since the torchlight days of William Jennings Bryan."[2] The election outcome "demonstrated that everyone accepted the rules but Harry S. Truman. He defied them. And he won."[3]

According to press accounts, the main factors contributing to Truman's surprise election victory included: a traditional reluctance to change leaders when the economy was stable, a supposed adherence to New Deal principles that was deeper than expected, negative feelings toward the "do-nothing" Eightieth Congress, particularly in regard to inflation, a strong turnout by labor, the overwhelming African American vote directed in Truman's favor, Truman's tough, hard-hitting, issues-oriented campaign, his personal warmth, and a decided sympathy for the underdog. By contrast, Dewey seemed reticent to tackle the issues, appeared aloof, and, in fact, seemed a bit arrogant.[4]

Certainly the coalition of farmers, African Americans, laborers, small business owners, and unhappy consumers aided Truman in his quest for the presidency. The president pounded hard on the farm issues, and many attributed the farm vote, in particular, to Truman's unexpected victory.[5] The *New York Times* attributed Truman's victory to support from farm states and big cities.[6] Campaign historian Gary Donaldson argues that part of the reason why Truman won the election was that the liberal-black-urban northern coalition had been enabled by the purgation of the racist South. With the Dixiecrats occupying the extreme right and the Progressives the more extremist realms of the left, Truman could occupy the more moderate center, a place that ultimately helped him win the day.[7]

Two groups deserve further commentary in this context—African Americans and labor organizations. Harry Truman's stance on civil rights had helped him with the African American vote. Although he addressed civil rights in detail only once during the campaign, election results revealed that Truman had carried the African American vote in the large cities by a wide margin. This development also led Donaldson to conclude "the votes of African Americans were probably the most important aspect of Truman's victory."[8] Labor employed its considerable forces to provide people for voter registration campaigns, and the unions made sure voters actually arrived at the polls. They also provided cars for the motorcades, drove dignitaries to various whistle-stops, and worked diligently to ensure that the turnout for the various rallies was substantial. Thus, labor played a key role in building the liberal-black-urban northern coalition that had led to Truman's victory.[9] While a coalition of groups certainly helped Truman deliver the vote, lively debate remains in the political literature over which particular segment of the coalition was most instrumental in Truman's upset victory. From a rhetorical vantage point, however, it is possible to amass some cohesive explanations.

Many had underestimated the president's political savvy and political pluck. Truman was a man who was part of the Great Depression. As part of an era of recent memory of suffering and want and New Deal measures to nullify the pain, the president's populist appeals still had merit because Americans had seen for themselves how much and how fast and how devastatingly prosperity could make its retreat. Truman prospered by rehearsing all the potential threats to prosperity and by associating Republicans with those whose greed for profit put others in harm's way. It was a discourse that would not return to the public sphere in quite the same way ever again. Truman represented a liberalism of a bygone era. In 1948, Truman's brand of liberalism still had a capacity to move and speak to the people.

Along with the populist appeals documented in this study, Truman provided engaged audiences with some very compelling reasons to support his presidential bid. Rhetorical constructions of character and personal narratives helped the president make persuasive inroads. Even questionable rhetorical tactics were factors in his success.

Character: A Winning Factor

Part of Truman's rhetorical success in the 1948 campaign had to do with the *persona* he projected. Surprisingly fit at age sixty-four, Harry S. Truman brought energy and passionate commitment to a campaign that left admirers and even his opponents in a state of awe, if not shock. His wit and simple, straightforward approach to the issues gained him a number of followers. Many wondered how the president could keep such a pace and, perhaps even more extraordinarily, do so with such a generousness of spirit. Not one person could remember a cantankerous chief executive beginning or ending a typical day on the campaign trail.

Truman was Everyman in the 1948 campaign. A consummate midwesterner, he could draw from his experience as a farmer, retailer, veteran, Shriner, and Mason. As the *New York Times* noted, "Mr. Truman could be the composite American of 1948."[10] Truman's public *ethos* was a key to his success. The particular attributes Truman offered were demonstrably accessible and attractive. As Kansas City journalist H. I. Phillips commented, "I size Harry Truman up as a pretty sound, careful, prudent, non-acrobatic, fairly old-fashioned American whose Missouri background and training will keep him from going haywire. I see him as a horse-sense individual, with much of the pioneer love of traditional American ways." What distinguished Truman from his opponent and made him an attractive candidate was his ability to convey to people that he was and remained "an instinctive believer in the American way, the plain folksy American of the town meeting, the cracker barrel, and the church supper. Out there in Missouri they believe in the 'Stop, Look, and Listen' and the 'Look Before You Leap' signs." Here was a man whose ego never outran his abilities and whose abilities surprised those with greater egos. His honesty, integrity, and solid homespun virtues were on display for all to see and people trusted him as a "solid American": "I think Harry's hat still fits and that above all he still likes to plow a straight furrow, and that always in his ear he hears his beloved mom whispering, 'Behave yourself, Harry.'"[11] Truman's sincerity and unpretentiousness enabled him to achieve a unique identification with the common citizen. According to another Kansas City journalist, W. L. White, who seemed disenchanted with Truman's victory, "The ordinary run of folks did it [elected Truman]. They felt he was one of them. Maybe he wasn't too smart, but they could see that he was sincere. They knew he had tried his best to be a good president for all the country, they like him and that was why they were willing last Tuesday to throw their votes away."[12]

Part of Truman's magic was his ability to dispense wisdom in clear and concise terms. Truman's aphorisms were not only familiar to the common citizen, by employing them he displayed a common touch that made common sense and established common ground. On October 6 in Lexington, Kentucky, Truman declared, "It's the horse that comes out ahead at the finish that counts." Even though he was president, he ran like a man with the odds stacked against him. His analogy fit both the region and his political circumstances, and it made him even more believable: "I am trying to do in politics what Citation has done in the horse races. I propose at the finish line on November 2 to come out ahead." Another aphorism was employed to rally listeners in Indianapolis on October 15: "Republicans don't like people to talk about depressions. . . . You remember the old saying: Don't talk about rope in the house of somebody who has been hanged."[13] The home-grown analogies and aphorisms were easily digested and understood.

Finally, as John Franklin Carter (pen name Jay Franklin), who served as a speechwriter for Truman on the whistle-stop tour, has noted, "Harry S. Truman believed in God and trusted the American people.... It was peculiarly Harry Truman's campaign and it reflected his character. Yet to bring that character into tune with the public will required an effort which was also a miracle of timing, calculation, and faith in democracy." Rhetorically, Truman "had no pride of authorship or opinion. But he had a Lincolnian talent for simplifying an idea and expressing it in terms familiar to the people he addressed."[14] As Zachary Karabell indicates, Truman's simple rhetorical style paid dividends: "Truman did not offer poetic rhetoric to the millions who heard one of his 280 speeches in the 30 states he passed through. He did not talk of grand philosophical themes along his 20,000 mile route, and he did not dwell on lofty ideas. Everywhere he went he attacked the Republicans for the high cost of living and painted the Democrats as the party of the people. He also varied the message and tailored his remarks to fit the place."[15] In this way, Truman differentiated himself from Thomas E. Dewey. Toward the end of the campaign, Eben Ayers, genuinely puzzled by all the predictions of a Dewey victory, would write in his diary: "I have repeatedly asked my wife how it is possible that the American people will vote for a man whom nobody likes and who tells them nothing."[16] It turned out that the public was asking itself the same question by campaign's end.

Simply put, then, Thomas E. Dewey was not as attractive a candidate as Harry S. Truman. The whistle-stop train tour helped uncover that fact. If Dewey was perceived as the cold organization man whose verbalizations were just a little too smooth and a bit too abstract all in the service of corporate and special interests, Truman could perhaps best define and contrast himself as a feisty, sometimes fuming Everyman whose concrete proposals and homespun values were crafted solely in the interest and the welfare of the people. Since Truman displayed characteristics of background and temperament people could readily identify with, it was easier to accept his appeals. Because people identified with the messenger, they were also able to identify with the message. Truman's ethos was one earned by the persona he projected on the campaign trail. Thus, one reason for the generation of positive attitudes and feelings comes from Truman's ability to evoke a clear image expressing a salient and consistent character.

Family Tree, Failure, and Hardscrabble Persistence

The president also demonstrated an ability to tap into an American narrative that had high resonance with many voters. He had an instinct for the importance of family, for roots, for identifying with his constituents whenever possible, linking his background with theirs. He came across as a friend or neighbor, an uncle telling the family tales with a bit too much corny relish but engaging all the same. This kind of encounter with Truman surprised some in his audience. A whistle-stop appearance in Shelbyville, Kentucky, demonstrates how Truman could spin a tale of family history that invited the constituents in a particular locality to view him as a person with a background much like theirs. He often would make direct familial links when and where possible:

My grandfather Truman ran off with Mary Jane Holmes and was married here in Shelbyville, and lived on an adjoining farm out here west of town. Then he went to Missouri—was afraid to go back home. And about 3 or 4 years after that, why his father-in-law sent for him to come home, he wanted to see the first grandchild. That settled things and they got together, and my grandfather Young and grandmother Young lived right around here. My grandmother was the youngest of 13 children, and they lived out here on the farm between here and Louisville. The house sat half in Jefferson County and half in Shelby County, and when my grandmother's brother—she was raised by her oldest brother—didn't want to serve on the jury in Jefferson County, he would move over to Shelby County, and when he didn't want to serve in Shelby County, he moved to Jefferson—he was very conveniently fixed.

I am proud of my Kentucky ancestry, naturally. Kentucky and Missouri are just symbolic of the ancestry there. Missouri was settled by people from Kentucky and Tennessee mostly, and the central part of Missouri from St. Louis to Kansas City is just a cross-section of Kentuckians, so I know exactly what you think about, and how you like things. If you will come out to Jackson County, I will show you a slice of Kentucky.[17]

In addition to the individual, familial, and territorial identifications, the president's own sense of the history of the nation comes through in this passage, which perhaps brought voters some additional comfort.

One pundit also noticed what seemed to be a Truman trademark in a whistle-stop speech. Truman "was the soul of modesty every time he touched on the tangled affairs of the Truman tribe. Truman seemed to take a perverse delight in recounting in great detail the hard-luck story of the Trumans."[18] There was not much mystery about this approach. On opening his campaign Labor Day weekend, Truman took to the back platform in Toledo and remarked:

Most of you people are working people, just as I have been all my life. I have had to work for everything I ever received. I never went into a political campaign in my life that I didn't have a fight to obtain what I thought was real and for the benefit of the people.

I have only been defeated once and that was for township committeeman in Washington Township in Missouri, back in 1912.

It does you a lot of good, sometimes, to understand just exactly what defeat means. In 1940 I had the bitterest campaign for reelection to the United States Senate that I think any man had in the history of this country. I had every newspaper in the State against me, the Governor of the State and his organization was against me, and at 11 o'clock that night, all the radio broadcasters and the papers said that I was defeated by 11,000 votes. I went to bed, got up next morning and found out I had been nominated, which was equivalent to election by more than 8,000 votes. I knew just exactly what it feels like to be defeated for major office. I don't want to have that experience this time. I would like to go to bed elected on November 2nd.[19]

Here the character and distinctiveness of Truman's populist appeals stand in clear relief. The president not only identifies with the struggle of the common man, he portrays *himself* as a lifelong "working man." The implied agony of his defeat in 1912 and his improbable and difficult Senate election campaign in 1940 provides demonstrable rhetorical proof of his mettle and his ability to overcome adversity. His narrative account also appeals to an American sense of individual achievement as well as our penchant for cheering those willing to pull themselves up by their own bootstraps and overcome hard times. These homespun virtues have resonance and credibility. By recounting his feelings after defeat and his elation at an unexpected win, Truman's narrative helps frame and influence the voters' choice for the upcoming election. Evoking sympathy and demonstrating tenacity, Truman trumpets his underdog status while remaining true to the designated campaign strategy.

The president's narrative references to his family helped audiences to understand that he was one of them and that he, like them, was not immune to adversity. He was from a family of working men and women who suffered all the vicissitudes that entails. His personal family history was introduced as a quintessentially American history—part and parcel of what it means to struggle to make a living and a life in America. The president's narratives were replete with stories of his grandfather who served as a freighter between Kansas City and the West Coast who had to sell his California ranch to pay off his many creditors. An uncle who ranched in Texas was ruined by the railroads' exorbitant shipping charges for transporting cattle to Kansas City. The Shelbyville train-side talk assured audiences of his roots and rootedness. It seemed important that Truman's grandfather hailed from Kentucky and eloped with a pretty girl from the neighborhood, and the audience smiled knowingly while the president sheepishly implied that his relatives had created quite a "ruckus." In the end, the newlyweds were finally forgiven and invited back home. The tales contained life's lessons and were woven from a common social fabric that was readily identified and appreciated.

These homespun stories on the campaign trail were transformed into the American story. Truman reintroduced Americans to themselves, and it provided a comforting identification. Truman's catalog of successes and failures, his easy manner, his optimistic attitude all conspired as one news account (written immediately after the election) put it, "to show that by family inheritance and by his own experience (as a failed farmer and haberdasher) that he was inured to the whips and lashes of fate, and that he could take defeat in his stride." But, "when Harry Truman, after failing at farming and merchandising, went quickly from county judge to Senator to Vice President to president, he had hit the biggest political jackpot in American history. And now he has hit the jackpot again."[20]

Identification with the common man, discussion of hard-luck stories, and dogged perseverance through a variety of forms of adversity also served as a rhetorical thematic counterpoint to Truman's own perceived underdog status. Truman was quite aware of the sentiment in the nation. A wily and intelligent political strategist in his own right, Truman used his presumed inferior status to his advantage. If he had the image of a bumbler in foreign policy, and if perhaps he seemed a little too loyal to cronies, and if his leadership was impugned, sometimes on a daily basis, then he resolved to take his case to the people because he firmly believed that if he personally brought his arguments to the court of public opinion he would be exonerated. Truman embarked on a one-man crusade to undo the negative images. He seemed confident that when folks met him in person the false images would recede. He did not act like an underdog, and he never showed any signs he was about to undergo what all the pundits and pollsters had almost unanimously predicted would be a humiliating, crushing defeat. In this respect, the president's argument was his ethos, and this ethos was drawn from his sincere and undeniable personification of the experience of a sizable number of Americans.

Questionable Rhetorical Tactics

Over the course of the campaign, Truman employed a variety of colorful, if not questionable, rhetorical tactics. He tore into the Republican "unity" campaign theme with a vengeance. In Philadelphia on October 6, he said, "We believe in the unity of free men. We believe in the unity of great causes. We don't believe in the unity of slaves or the unity of sheep being led to slaughter." In Rochester, New York, on October 8 he implied that the Republicans were deceiving the people with their appeals to unity: "The [GOP] leopard has not changed its spots—he has merely hired some public relations experts. And they have taught him to wear sheep's clothing and purr sweet nothings about unity in a soothing voice. But it's the same old leopard." Truman could add a humorous touch to these attacks from time to time. In Boston on October 27 Truman declared, "Now the Republicans tell me that they stand for unity. In the old days Al Smith would have said: 'That's baloney.' Today the Happy Warrior would say: 'That's a lot of hooey!' And if that rhymes with anything, it is not my fault."

The president employed name-calling and stinging metaphors to rouse his audience to attention. In Detroit on Labor Day, he had spared the Republicans little by way of brickbats. He charged that the typical Republican was a "shrewd man with a calculating machine where his heart ought to be." In Dexter, Iowa, he had labeled the opposition "gluttons of privilege" who would return the nation to the days of "Wall Street economic dictatorship." And even more infamously, he referred to the Eightieth "do-nothing" Congress, which had "already stuck a pitchfork in the farmers back." He complained that the gains for farmers removed by past Republican greed would only pale in comparison to what they would do with a victory in 1948; their voracious appetites were only "an appetizer for the economic tapeworm of big business." He tarnished the GOP as a party of "old mossbacks," who tried "lulling the public to sleep" with "high level platitudes." The metaphors seemed a tad dated and tired, even at the time, but Truman spoke with conviction and there was no mistaking his political targets.

Although his manner of reasoning was down home and connected with people, Truman was not above employing common fallacies in his appeals. In Los Angeles at Gilmore Stadium on September 23, Truman charged that if the nation were to fall into Republican hands, just about "everything is likely to be all wrong within a very short time." This "slippery slope" argument is a classic textbook example of what argumentation theorists and philosophers label fallacious reasoning. A statement made in St. Paul, Minnesota, on October 13 reveals another example of fallacious reasoning: "The Republican Party either corrupts its liberals or it expels them." Such either-or reasoning closes down options and directs audiences to hasty conclusions.

As we have seen previously, Truman was not above an old-fashioned personal attack against an opponent. On September 28 in Marietta, Oklahoma, the president commented on the retirement of Republican Senator Edward H. Moore as follows: "I'm glad Ole Man Moore is quitting. Ole Man Moore was never any good anyway."[21] In back-platform whistle-stop remarks on October 8 in Auburn, New York, Truman issued another blistering personal attack on Republican anti–New Deal conservative John Taber: "I am sorry to say that your Congressman from this district has used a butcher knife and a sabre and a meat-axe on the appropriations that have been in the public interest both for the farmers, for rural electrification, and for every other forward-looking program that has come before Congress. I saw a cartoon the other day called 'The Sabre Dance,' in which they showed a big man with a sabre cutting the heads off all the appropriation for the Interior Department and the Department of Agriculture. Well, I have a better name than that. I named it 'The Taber Dance.'"[22] Thus, Truman's use of humor could be biting as well as entertaining for partisans.

Truman's most controversial rhetorical activity, eclipsing both the divisive Detroit Labor Day speech and the stinging Dexter, Iowa, address, occurred on October 25 in a major speech in Chicago. In a blatant attempt to compare the Republican Party to the Nazis, Truman stated, "In our own time, we've seen the tragedy of the Italian and German peoples, who lost their freedom to men who made promises of unity and efficiency and security. . . . When a few men get control of the economy of the nation, they find a 'front' man to run the country for them." It was clear that the Republicans were calling for unity, had praised Thomas E. Dewey's efficiency, and had been charged by Truman with representing the special interests and lobbies to the detriment of the common citizen. Thus, the "front" man for the wealthy Wall Street elite inescapably pointed to the Republican presidential candidate. But equating the Republicans with the Nazis went beyond "tough" political discourse. It was a scurrilous and unfounded charge. Not only was this a false analogy, it was a slur that besmirched the office of the presidency and should have been scrupulously avoided.[23]

This brief survey of questionable rhetorical appeals begs a larger a question—whether or not, on the whole, Truman conducted a demagogic political campaign. Such a question, of course, poses a dilemma. Was Truman exploiting the people for personal gain, or was he merely conveying what he thought was best for the nation and framing the issues accordingly? From the point of view of rhetorical judgment and assessment, it is clear that Truman engaged at times in questionable rhetorical tactics, but there is less evidence for building a concerted or coherent pattern of deceit or deception, and still less evidence for drawing the conclusion that Truman spoke merely from self-interest, which is often the hallmark of the demagogue.

A more compelling explanation for Truman's rhetoric and its effectiveness can be traced to the simple fact that he employed a populist discourse that offended some and energized others. Analysis of Truman's major speeches and whistle-stop remarks has revealed that he used a combination of populist themes to portray himself as the only candidate who could defend ordinary Americans from exploitation by the self-serving and privileged elite. Often mirroring populist rhetoric redolent of late-nineteenth-century America, which emphasized themes of impending powerlessness for the masses, Truman saddled Republicans with victimizing farmers, laborers, and small businesspersons alike. He pointed to the tangible benefits that the Democratic Party had won for the common man, and he portrayed his opponents as the unwarranted usurpers of wealth and privilege who served elite lobbies and interests. Periods of Republican control were identified with exploitation of the people and a disregard for the common interest. He evoked painful public memories of Republican governance that led to the Great Depression, generating fear and uneasiness: "You remember the Hoover cart—the remains of the Old Tin Lizzie being pulled by a mule because you couldn't afford to buy a new car or gas for the old one. You remember. First you had the Hoovercrats and then you had the

Hoover carts. One always follows the other."[24] Finally, Truman depicted his own candidacy as a primary means of continuing democratic ideals and defending the ordinary citizen from harm, intentional abuse, and continued political and economic exploitation.

In portraying himself as a common man for the common good, Truman found a theme and a voice. His overt, personal populism was part and parcel of a historical and rhetorical strand in the American political culture—that of defending the "little people." No doubt Truman exploited this theme to his advantage. While he sometimes seemed to teeter on the precipice with the likes of Pitchfork "Ben" Tillman and Huey Long, once he made his populist commitments known, he never backed down. As a *New York Times* editorial suggested, "Some parts of his campaign were in bad taste. Often he seemed to be talking the language of William J. Bryan and of 1896 rather than of post-war America in 1948. Yet his audiences appeared to gain a sense of direction from him."[25] At question is how Truman was able to provide "a sense of direction" without simultaneously reverting to a demagogic campaign.

In his recorded public and private musings Truman indicated that his policy pronouncements were linked to sacrosanct democratic principles. As he wrote in his memoirs, "The platform of a political party is a promise to the public. Unless a man can run on his party's platform—and try to carry it out, if elected—he is not an honest man. All campaign oratory that is not based on principles and issues represented in a definite platform is sheer demagoguery. When a party has no principles and issues on which to stand, it invariably turns to personalities and to the use of the 'big lie' technique, ignoring the only basis upon which a political campaign can be logically conducted."[26] Truman was never inconsistent in this regard. His campaign rhetoric closely followed and supported the Democratic Party platform. He discussed the issues and challenged his Republican opponents to do likewise. Upon occasion, Truman was rightfully accused of employing suspect rhetorical means, but his ends were generally unassailable—at least by the standards of his own party. So it seems clear that, in the long run, principle trumped expediency in Truman's campaign discourse.

The president fully believed that his allegiances and his pronouncements were synchronous. In his view, this was not the case with his opponents. Truman's relentless attacks against the Eightieth Congress and his call for a special session had to do with the fact that, in his judgment, through their pronounced inaction, the Republicans had run away from their platform and from the crucial problems that needed national solutions. For Truman, this was the height of hypocrisy, and he and his advisers designed his campaign as an effort to unmask it.

In sum, the evidence in this study suggests that Truman, upon occasion, did engage in demagogic rhetorical tactics. The public and the private record also suggest, however, that the president's primary motive was not tied to selfish interest and personal gain. While he admittedly stood to gain the White House and some selfish motives may have attended his rhetorical appeals, there is no reason to conclude that Truman routinely engaged his political craft during the 1948 campaign as a full-fledged, free-range, gun-toting, unreconstructed demagogue. Truman simply exercised a firmly held and effectively targeted version of populist persuasion.

Conclusion

When the campaign was finally over, the president estimated he had traveled over thirty thousand miles and delivered 356 speeches. He believed that twelve to fifteen million people had come out to see him.[27] As David McCullough observed, "No president in history had ever gone so far in quest of support from the people, or with less cause for the effort, to judge by informed opinion. Nor would any presidential candidate ever again attempt such a campaign by railroad."[28] When the president's locomotive passed through small towns and villages or when he traveled by motorcade to the great metropolises of this nation, his oratory seemed natural and unassuming. He had become a "man of the people."

It has been argued throughout this book that Harry S. Truman's discourse in the 1948 campaign displayed all the important characteristics of a populist rhetoric. Just as importantly, his public persona was built upon a life history and experience that embodied moral virtues critical to Truman's identification with his audience and the themes of his campaign. As a result, Truman's populist appeals seemed to be genuinely felt and they translated effectively to a well-targeted citizenry in both urban and rural settings. Whether the appeal was to workers in Detroit, farmers in Iowa, or to the African American diaspora in the post–World War II era, Truman found that his key themes struck a responsive cord in the crucial coalition he had rhetorically patched together over time. The resulting electoral quilt was enough to win an upset election.

Truman's polarized rhetoric helped reduce the campaign to a simple, almost unassailable decision. The choice he offered to the voters was clear because he allowed the audiences no room to supply their own answers; he offered the claims and supplied the verbalized warrants, leaving nothing to chance. The result was a clear, undiluted, simple message: "I think you understand the issues of this campaign; it's just the special interests against the people. And the Democrats stand for the people and the Republicans stand for the special interests." This populist message was repeated time and again.

Rhetorically, then, Truman left nothing for the audience to imagine or interpret; he supplied all the definitions and answered all the questions he posed. He trusted in his audience to see things the way he saw them, clear, circumspect, black and white, and right on the issues. He relied on his personal ethos to overcome the doubters. As he said in a campaign train stop in Lock Haven, Pennsylvania, on October 23: "You know there has been so much publicity about your President not knowing where he is going or what he is doing or anything of the kind that people are surprised when they find that he does know where he is going and knows what he is doing."[29]

Truman attributed his success on the whistle-stop train tour to his own firm grasp of the nation: "I was familiar with every section of the country, and I knew people in every section of the country, and naturally that's an asset to a politician."[30] His familiarity with a particular locale or region, his strategy of identifying local needs and linking them to national issues, his humor, and his sincerity, all played a role in making the whistle-stop tour a success. The train tour allowed Truman to present himself to the American people, voice their values, apprise them of the issues, and tailor his populist message to their interests. As Cole S. Brembeck notes, "The full impact of the whistle stop campaign hits one with sudden force when [one] listens to the President shape his appeals to fit the fears, wants, and loyalties of diverse interest groups in various parts of the country." Whether he addressed inflation, labor, a living wage, and the cost of housing in the North, farm price supports, corn, and the storage of grain in the Midwest, or public power, flood control, and cattle ranching in the West, Truman spoke specifically and plainly to the interests of the locality. According to Brembeck, simply put, "The self-interest appeals won votes for Truman."[31] But there was something more. As Truman biographer Alonzo Hamby notes, "The unexpected victory of the little guy over the organization man captured the imagination of much of the country. Seeming in some way to affirm the country's promise, it made Americans feel good about themselves."[32]

The whistle-stop train tour helped solidify Truman's political miracle, and the central feature of the tour was Truman's rhetoric. Campaign historian Gary Donaldson maintained that Truman's whistle-stops "had a significant impact on the outcome of the election." Indeed, "Through the whistle-stop tours, Truman made his face and personality visible to thousands of potential supporters in the last months of 1948, and it clearly made a difference."[33] Brembeck takes Donaldson's claim a step further: "The whistle stop campaign may have been *the deciding factor* in the Truman victory. One of the 'intangibles' in the election, its persuasive effect was little understood or appreciated" (emphasis added).[34]

In fact, Truman's personal rhetorical appeals and their effect on the populace were anything but peripheral to his success in the 1948 campaign. When the crowds met Truman on the back platform of the *Ferdinand Magellan* at the whistle-stops across America, they encountered a feisty optimist whose very visage bespoke a man who had pursued and realized the American dream. Truman's rhetorically defined persona countered the press's and his opponents' negative descriptions. The people who turned out on the hustings appreciated his energy, his candor, and his fighting, never-say-die spirit. His knowledge of the hamlets and small town America and his identification with the folks who came out to greet him at various and sundry times of day or night to dutifully assemble trackside forged the kind of intimate trust that only personal contact can engender. When he was at his best, Truman could deliver a disarmingly effective rhetorical performance. In major cities and at the whistle-stops, the citizens and their president both took home a piece of history. Their mutual encounter gave them a bit more hope in themselves and in their country. For many, it was simply bracing. As J. Jeffery Auer suggests, "there is no better way to explain the Democratic victory in 1948 than to say that an honest and forthright man of the people employed the power of appropriate and effective public speech to persuade the American electorate."[35]

Truman's rhetorical legacy is one that may not translate well in an electronic environment where television and the Internet now dominate the modern election. But Truman may yet have a few lessons for the sophisticated postmodern politician. At the very least, a focus on his campaign teaches us that there is no substitute for old-fashioned human contact. The wave and the handshake, the sound of the amplified voice over the loudspeaker, the flash of the camera, the rising chorus and spectacle of the political rally, the exchange of gifts between the citizenry and their candidate, and all the excitement and colorful hoopla of a presidential visit, especially to a small town, can still draw a crowd and draw a people together to once again help sort out how personal lives and destinies are conjoined with the outcome of a national election. The *Ferdinand Magellan* may have been retired to a museum, but its symbolic import will never be retired. The image of Truman's wide, satisfied grin as he held up the *Chicago Tribune* headline "Dewey Defeats Truman" while standing on the rear platform at the back of his personal train car will live in political lore as long as people's hopes and dreams attach themselves to the mythic strands of rebirth and regeneration a four-year election cycle always brings.

Notes

All unpublished documents cited are held in the Harry S. Truman Library, Independence, Missouri (abbreviated as Truman Library), unless otherwise noted.

Abbreviations

CHP = 1948 Campaign Broadcasts, Charter Heslep Papers, Truman Library.

CVF = 1948 Election Campaign Vertical File, Truman Library.

LCF = Democratic National Committee Library Clipping Files, Truman Library.

MPA = Motion Picture Archive, Truman Library.

PDF = Democratic National Committee Publicity Division Files, Truman Library.

PPP = *Public Papers of the Presidents of the United States: Harry S. Truman, 1945–1953,* Truman Library. Online Access, trumanlibrary .org.

PRM = 1948 Presidential Campaign, Post Mortems and Reference Material, Truman Library.

PSF = President's Secretary's Files, Truman Library.

RPO = Records of the American Institute of Public Opinion, Truman Library.

TCF = Truman Chronological File, Vertical File, Truman Library.

TMF = Truman Memoirs File, Truman Library.

Introduction

1. George M. Elsey, *An Unplanned Life,* 158.

Harry S. Truman's Rear-Platform Remarks in Decatur, Illinois

1. Rear-Platform and Other Informal Remarks in Indiana and Illinois, Decatur, Illinois (3:30 PM), Oct. 12, 1948, PPP, http://www.trumanlibrary.org/publicpapers/index.php?pid=1983&st=&st1.

Chapter 1. Setting the Political and Rhetorical Strategy, January–May 1948

1. James David Barber, *The Presidential Character*, 241.
2. Harold I. Gullan, *The Upset that Wasn't*, 44.
3. Memo, David K. Niles to Matthew Connelly, Oct. 8, 1946, Polls, PSF Political File, box 49.
4. Letter, Harry S. Truman to Russell Birdwell, Nov. 12, 1946, New York, PSF Political File, box 49.
5. Zachary Karabell, *The Last Campaign*, 87–88.
6. Memo, Clark Clifford to Harry S. Truman, Nov. 19, 1947, Clifford Papers, box 23. For a look at the original Rowe memorandum and Clifford's adaptation see "Analysis: The Politics of 1948," dated Sept. 18, 1947, from James Rowe Jr. to President Harry S. Truman; and "Memo," dated Nov. 19, 1947, from Clark M. Clifford, Special Counsel to President Harry S. Truman, to President Harry S. Truman, both available at http://www.trumanlibrary.org/whistle-stop/study_collections/1948campaign/large/docs/index.php. For a discussion of the specific origins and development of this famous memo, see Robert H. Ferrell, *Harry S. Truman: A Life*, 275. General references to this memo will be labeled as the Rowe-Clifford memorandum.
7. Memo, Clifford to Harry S. Truman, "The 1948 Campaign," Aug. 17, 1948; Confidential Memo to the President; Clifford-Rowe memo of Nov. 19, 1947 [1of 2]. Clifford Papers, box 22.
8. Cable, "United States Political Struggle Tends Toward Domestic Issues," July 31, 1947, Frantz—Subject File of Stories Filed By Harry W. Frantz 1948 Election Campaign—1947, Harry W. Frantz Papers, box 14.

9. Proposed Plan of Action by the President, Strategy-General, PSF Political File, box 50. Given the subjects discussed, it is likely the memo was developed prior to mid-May of 1948.
10. Robert A. Divine, "The Cold War and the Election of 1948," *Journal of American History* 59 (1972): 90–110. In July of 1948, Dewey decided to restrain his criticism of Truman's foreign policy when the Berlin blockade increased U.S.-Soviet tensions to the boiling point. Nevertheless, according to Divine, "The Cold War cast a long shadow over the election of 1948, influencing the campaign strategies of the rival candidates and shaping in a subtle but vital way the final outcome"(p. 91).
11. Foot-Notes on the Opportunities of the White House in the Political Battles of 1948, Strategy-General, PSF Political File, box 50.
12. "Tulsa Billboard," *Time*, Apr. 19, 1948, CVF (2).
13. "Summary of Remarks by George M. Elsey, Politics 203, Princeton University, January 11, 1949," 1948 Presidential Campaign Remarks by George M. Elsey Regarding 1948 Election, Speech File, Elsey Papers, box 32.
14. Gullan, *The Upset that Wasn't*, 5.
15. Informal remarks of the president to the members of the President's Committee on Civil Rights, Jan. 15, 1947, Civil Rights and Minorities, 1937–1947, Niles Papers, box 26. See Executive Order 9808 (3 CFR, 1943–1948 Comp., p. 590). The committee's report, titled "To Secure These Rights" (Washington, D.C.: Government Printing Office) was made public October 29, 1947. The importance of this report will be addressed in subsequent discussion.
16. Donald R. McCoy and Richard T. Ruetten, *Quest and Response,* 100, 103.
17. Address before the National Association for the Advancement of Colored People, June 29, 1947, PPP, http://trumanlibrary.org/publicpapers/index.php?pid=2115&st=&st1. For an excellent analysis of this address see Garth Pauley, "Harry Truman and the NAACP: A Case Study in Presidential Persuasion on Civil Rights," *Rhetoric & Public Affairs* 2 (1999): 211–41. This article was

reprinted as "Harry Truman and the NAACP," in Garth Pauley, *The Modern Presidency and Civil Rights*, 31–57.

18. Report, Motivation of Propaganda on Civil Liberties, July 17, 1947, Correspondence with Government Agencies: State Department, President's Committee on Civil Rights, box 6. For an argument that Truman's stance on civil rights was not politically motivated see Michael R. Gardner, *Harry Truman and Civil Rights*.

19. For three excellent assessments of the relationship between African American civil rights and Cold War diplomacy see John David Skrentny, "The Effect of the Cold War on African American Civil Rights: America and the World Audience, 1945–1968," *Theory and Society* 27 (1998): 237–85; Mary L. Dudziak, *Cold War Civil Rights*; Thomas Borstelmann, *The Cold War and the Color Line*.

20. Press Release, Statement by the President, Oct. 29, 1947, OF 596, box 1509.

21. For a fuller treatment of the activities and import of the President's Committee on Civil Rights see Steven R. Goldzwig, "Inaugurating the Second Reconstruction: President Truman's Committee on Civil Rights" in *Civil Rights Rhetoric and the American Presidency*, ed. James Arnt Aune and Enrique D. Rigsby, 83–113. For a look at the report as distributed by the commercial press see *"To Secure These Rights": The Report of the President's Committee on Civil Rights* (New York: Simon and Schuster, 1947).

22. Special Message to the Congress on Civil Rights, Feb. 2, 1948, PPP, http://trumanlibrary.org/publicpapers/index.php?pid =1380&st=&st1.

23. Wayne Fields, *Union of Words*, 40.

24. Karabell, *The Last Campaign*, 75.

25. Public Opinion News Service Releases, RPO, box 1.

26. George Gallup, "Truman Now Trailing Top Four Republican Candidates," *Washington Post*, Apr. 11, 1948, Gallup Polls, Clifford Papers, box 22.

27. Karabell, *The Last Campaign*, 88.

28. "Give 'em Hell, Harry!" No. 16 of the series "Decision: The

Conflicts of Harry S. Truman," 26 minutes, 1964, 16mm (on videotape), MPA, MP-81–6.

29. TMF. Clark Clifford takes credit for helping the president develop a strategy to take his case to the nation: "I recommended several long train tours of the nation, targeting specifically those states that had been most closely contested in 1944, especially California." This was Governor Earl Warren's home state. Clark Clifford, *Counsel to the President*, 226.

30. Ferrell. *Harry S. Truman: A Life*, 269.

31. Robert J. Donovan, *Conflict and Crisis*, 394.

32. Robert Underhill, *The Truman Persuasions*, 196.

33. Donald R. McCoy, *The Presidency of Harry S. Truman*, 153.

34. Harry S. Truman, *Memoirs of Harry S. Truman: Years of Trial and Hope, 1946–1952*, vol. 2, 179.

Chapter 2. The Western Tour, June 1948

1. "Mr. Truman Takes to the Road," editorial, June 4, 1948, Editorials, June–Oct. 1948, *Congressional Quarterly* Newspaper Clipping File, box 1.

2. "Nonpolitical, Say Aides of Truman Trip," *Washington Post*, June 2, 1948, Pre-Campaign Trip, June 3, 1948–June 18, 1948, Murphy Files, box 1.

3. Memorandum on Train Trip, June 3, 1948, Ferdinand Magellan Railroad Car, Truman Subject File, Vertical File.

4. Rear Platform Remarks in Ohio and Indiana, June 4, 1948, Crestline, Ohio (12 PM), PPP, http://trumanlibrary.org/public papers/index.php?pid=1643&st=&st1.

5. Donovan, *Conflict and Crisis*, 396.

6. Address in Chicago before the Swedish Pioneer Centennial Association, PPP, http://trumanlibrary.org/publicpapers/index .php?pid=1644&st=&st1.

7. Summary of President Truman's Western Trip, June 3–18, 1948, PSF, box 7.

8. Ibid.

9. Press Clippings, Niel Johnson, "The Day Omaha Turned Its Back," *Sunday World Herald Magazine of the Midlands*, Oct. 24, 1976, CVF (4).

10. Ibid.

11. Summary of President Truman's Western Trip.

12. Donovan, *Conflict and Crisis*, 397.

13. Summary of President Truman's Western Trip.

14. Ibid.

15. Press Clippings, "Whistle-Stop," CVF (1).

16. Correspondence-Clippings, Chairman, 1947–1949, "Democrats Turn 'Whistle-Stop' Gag against Taft," *[Washington?] Times-Herald*, June 20, 1948, Democratic National Committee Records, McGrath Papers, box 61.

17. Summary of President Truman's Western Trip.

18. Alonzo L. Hamby, *Man of the People*, 443.

19. Elsey, *An Unplanned Life*, 163.

20. Rear-Platform and Other Informal Remarks in Washington, Everett, Washington (Rear platform, 7:50 PM), June 9, 1948, PPP, http://trumanlibrary.org/publicpapers/index.php?pid=1658&st=&st1.

21. Summary of President Truman's Western Trip.

22. Ibid.

23. Commencement Address at the University of California, June 12, 1948, PPP, http://trumanlibrary.org/publicpapers/index.php?pid=1674&st=&st1.

24. Summary of President Truman's Western Trip.

25. Donovan, *Conflict and Crisis*, 399.

26. Karabell, *The Last Campaign*, 137.

27. "Summary of Remarks by George M. Elsey in Politics 203, Princeton University, January 11, 1949," 1948 Presidential Campaign Remarks by George M. Elsey at Princeton Regarding the 1948 Election, Elsey Papers, box 32.

28. Letter, Oscar L. Chapman to Paul D. Shriver, 1948 Campaign P–Z, Chapman Papers, box 84.

29. Clifford, *Counsel to the President*, 226.

30. Edward Rogge, "The Miracle of '48—Twenty-Six Years in Forming," *Southern Speech Journal* 25 (1960): 264–72, esp. 268.
31. Summary of President Truman's Western Trip.
32. Letter, Oscar Chapman to James C. Quigley, June 23, 1948, California Trip—Presidential, Chapman Papers, box 84.

Chapter 3. The Democratic National Convention
and the Special Session of Congress, July 1948

1. Irwin Ross, *The Loneliest Campaign,* 116–19.
2. Gary A. Donaldson, *Truman Defeats Dewey,* 187.
3. William C. Berman, *The Politics of Civil Rights in the Truman Administration,* 106–107; originally quoted in the *New York Times,* July 6, 1948, p. 26.
4. Berman, *The Politics of Civil* Rights, 111.
5. Ibid., 112.
6. Ibid., 112–13.
7. Ernest K. Lindley, "Democratic Low Ebb," *Newsweek,* July 19, 1948, Magazine Articles on President, Folder 1, LCF, Box 35.
8. Ross, *The Loneliest Campaign,* 130–31. According to Ross, Truman later boasted improbably that he was responsible for and endorsed the strengthened civil rights plank (see p. 126).
9. "National Party Platforms," CVF (3).
10. Memo, William L. Batt to Clark M. Clifford, July 9, 1948, July 15, 1948 Acceptance Speech before the Democratic National Convention, Philadelphia, Pennsylvania, Presidential Speech File, Clifford Papers, box 33.
11. "Give 'Em Hell, Harry!" video.
12. Address in Philadelphia upon Accepting the Nomination of the Democratic National Convention, July 15, 1948, *Public Papers of the Presidents: Harry S. Truman, 1945–1953,* HSTL, http://truman-library.org/publicpapers/index.php?pid =1060&st=&st1. Recalling Congress into special session had precedent, but it had not been exercised since 1856 when Pres. Franklin Pierce convened

the Senate and the House to secure additional military funding. See Karabell, *The Last Campaign*, 160. In calling Congress back into session on "Turnip Day," the president employed a homespun reference. Missouri farmers had an old adage: "on the 25th of July, / Sow your turnips wet or dry." Since July 25 was a Sunday, the president would call Congress back into session on Monday, July 26, "wet or dry." See Ferrell, *Harry S. Truman: A Life*, 270. For a look at Truman at work delivering his acceptance speech see "Give 'Em Hell, Harry!" video. For an additional analysis of the rhetorical strategies associated with Truman's nomination convention address see Halford R. Ryan, *Harry S. Truman*, 89–99.

13. Raymond P. Brandt, "Truman Special Session Call is Daring Gamble," *St. Louis Post-Dispatch*, July 16, 1948, 1948 Campaign Clippings, LCF, box 32.

14. "Dewey's Strategy vs. The President's," Aug. 1948, OF 299-E, box 947.

15. Memo, William L. Batt Jr. to Clark M. Clifford, July 22, 1948, Miscellaneous—Political File, 1948, [1 of 2], Clifford Papers, box 21.

16. Fields, *Union of Words*, 95.

17. Executive Order 9980 relating to fair employment practices in the Federal service and Executive Order 9981 establishing the President's Committee on Equality of Treatment and Opportunity in the Armed Services can be located at 3 CFR, 1943–1948 Comp., pp. 720, 722. Full realization of the desegregation of U.S. armed forces was not accomplished until the Korean War. See Steven R. Goldzwig "Civil Rights and the Cold War: A Rhetorical History of the Truman Administration and the Desegregation of the United States Army" in *Doing Rhetorical History: Concepts and Cases*, ed. Kathleen Turner, 143–69; Berman, *The Politics of Civil Rights*.

18. Donovan, *Conflict and Crisis*, 415.

19. Edward T. Folliard, "President Calls Session a Failure," *Washington Post*, undated, 1948 Campaign Clippings, LCF, box 37.

Chapter 4. The Fall Campaign Begins, September 1948

1. "Mr. Truman Intends to Fight," editorial, *Washington Star*, Aug. 19, 1948, 1948 Campaign Clippings, LCF, box 32.
2. "President Truman's 1948 Campaign Speaking Appearances," CVF (1).
3. "Description of Motorcade," Pittsburgh, Pa., Oct. 23, 1948, Harry S. Truman 1948 Campaign Speeches, Oct. 12–23, 1948, CHP, box 1.
4. For a thorough and informative look at Truman's speechwriting team and the speechwriting process see Diana B. Carlin, "Harry S. Truman: From Whistle-Stops to the Halls of Congress" in *Presidential Speechwriting: From the New Deal to the Reagan Revolution and Beyond*, ed. Kurt Ritter and Martin J. Medhurst, 40–67, and Underhill, *The Truman Persuasions*, esp. 157–208.
5. Charles S. Murphy Oral History, interviewed by C. T. Morrissey, May 2, 1963.
6. See for example, "Remarks," Rock Island, Ill., Sept. 18, 1948, PSF, box 1; "Remarks," Cayuga, N.Y., Oct. 8, 1948, PSF, box 2; "Remarks," Rochester, Minn., Oct. 14, 1948, PSF, box 2; Sample Outline for Short Speech, Campaign Trip #2, Western Tour, Murphy Files, box, 1.
7. Johannes Hoeber Oral History, interviewed by Jerry N. Hess, Washington, D.C., Sept. 13, 1966.
8. Letter, George M. Elsey to Charles S. Murphy, Sept. 25, 1948, Campaign Trip #3, Murphy Files, box 2.
9. Press Clippings, Charles G. Ross, "How Truman Did It," *Colliers*, Dec. 25, 1948, CVF(4).
10. Robert C. McMath Jr., *American Populism*, 111–12, 182, 187.
11. Michael Kazin, *The Populist Persuasion*, 1.
12. Ibid., 1–2.
13. Lloyd Rohler, "Conservative Appeals to the People: George Wallace's Populist Rhetoric," *Southern Communication Journal* 64 (1999): 316–22; quotation, 316–17.
14. Kazin, *The Populist Persuasion*; Rohler, "Conservative Appeals," 317.

15. Rohler, "Conservative Appeals."
16. Ronald Lee, "The New Populist Campaign for Economic Democracy: A Rhetorical Exploration," *Quarterly Journal of Speech* 72 (1986): 274–89; quotation, 274.
17. Steven R. Goldzwig, "A Social Movement Perspective on Demagoguery: Achieving Symbolic Realignment," *Communication Studies* 40 (1989): 202–28.
18. J. Michael Hogan and Glen Williams, "The Rusticity and Religiosity of Huey P. Long," *Rhetoric & Public Affairs* 7 (2004): 149–72; quotation, 151.
19. Hogan and Williams, "The Rusticity and Religiosity," 166.
20. Underhill, *The Truman Persuasions*, 182.
21. Robert J. Donovan, "Truman to Open Drive with Five Speeches Today," *New York Herald-Tribune*, Sept. 6, 1948, President Truman's Trip to Detroit, Michigan For Labor Day Speech, Sept. 5–7, 1948, Trip File, Michigan, OF 200–2-H.
22. The American Federation of Labor made its first formal entry into a presidential campaign in 1948 on the heels of the Democratic losses in the midterm elections and the subsequent inability of labor forces to deliver enough votes to stave off the Taft-Hartley Act. Even as Truman railed against the act, it was clear that a majority of Americans supported its provisions. This set of circumstances reinforces labor's importance. Press Clippings, Joseph C. Goulden, "'Give 'em Hell, Harry,'" *Washington Post*, July 25, 1976, CVF (2). For a defense of the Taft-Hartley Act see "Mr. Truman Opens a Campaign," editorial, *New York Times*, Sept. 7, 1948, 1948 Presidential Campaign, President's Labor Day Speeches, Sept. 6, 1948, Elsey Papers, box 24.
23. Labor Address in Cadillac Square, Detroit, Sept. 6, 1948, PPP, http://trumanlibrary.org/publicpapers/index.php?pid=1798&st=&st1.
24. See, for example, Newspaper Clipping, "Era of Fear," Sept. 7, 1948, 1948 Presidential Campaign, President's Labor Day Speeches, Sept. 6, 1948, Elsey Papers, box 24; Joseph M. Short, "Truman Sees 'Era of Fear' if GOP Wins," *Baltimore Sun*, Sept. 7, 1948, Labor Day Speeches, LCF, box 32; Felix Belair Jr., "President Warns of

an Era of Fear: Urges Heavy Vote," *New York Times*, Sept. 7, 1948, 1948 Presidential Campaign, President's Labor Day Speeches, Sept. 6, 1948, Elsey Papers, box 24.

25. Attachment to Letter, Herb Plambeck to Charles G. Ross, Sept. 11, 1948, OF 200–2-H, box 752.
26. Press Clippings, Joseph C. Goulden, "Give 'em Hell, Harry," *Washington Post*, July 25, 1976, CVF (2).
27. Ferrell, *Harry S. Truman: A Life*, 277.
28. Address at Dexter, Iowa, on the Occasion of the National Plowing Match, Sept. 18, 1948, PPP, http://trumanlibrary.org/publicpapers/index.php?pid=1814&st=&st1.
29. Donovan, *Conflict and Crisis*, 421–22.
30. Clifford, *Counsel to the President*, 228.
31. Rear-Platform and Other Informal Remarks in California and Arizona. Oceanside, California, 10:45 AM, Sept. 24, 1948, PPP, http://trumanlibrary.org/publicpapers/index.php?pid=1956&st=&st1.
32. Rear-Platform Remarks in California, Sept. 23, 1948, PPP, http://trumanlibrary.org/publicpapers/index.php?pid=1954&st=&st1.
33. President Harry Truman Reception, Gilmore Stadium, Thursday, Sept. 23, 1948, Program 6:00–10:00 PM, Trip File, California, Los Angeles, OF 200–2H.
34. Address at Gilmore Stadium, Los Angeles, CA, Sept. 23, 1948, PPP, http://trumanlibrary.org/publicpapers/index.php?pid=1955&st=&st1.
35. President Harry Truman Reception, Gilmore Stadium.
36. W. H. Lawrence, "Communists Guide Wallace's Party, Truman Declares," *New York Times*, Sept. 24, 1948, Speech at Los Angeles, Calif., Sept. 23, LCF, Politics/Campaign Speeches, 1948, box 32.
37. Charter Heslep Letters to Wife, 9–48–3–49, Western Union Press Message, Sept. 20, 1948, CHP, box 2.
38. Rear-Platform Remarks, Colton, Calif. (1:56 PM), Sept. 24, 1948, PPP, http://trumanlibrary.org/publicpapers/index.php?pid=1956&st=&st1.
39. Ibid.
40. Karabell, *The Last Campaign*, 214.
41. Joseph Driscoll, "Truman Returns to Washington, Meets 'Surprise' Demonstration," *St. Louis Post-Dispatch*, Oct. 2, 1948, Return to

Washington, D.C., after Western Trip, Oct. 2, 1948, LCF, Politics/ Campaign Speeches, 1948, box 34.

42. Dorthea Andrews, "Crowd Greets Truman on His Return Here," *Washington Post*, Oct. 3, 1948, Return to Washington, D.C., after Western Trip, Oct. 2, 1948, LCF, Politics/Campaign Speeches, 1948, box 34; W. H. Lawrence, "Truman, Back, Sees Fight Just Begun," *New York Times*, Oct. 3, 1948, Return to Washington, D.C., after Western Trip, Oct. 2, 1948, LCF, Politics/Campaign Speeches, 1948, box 34.

43. Anthony Leviero, "Up-State to Hear Truman This Week," *New York Times*, Oct. 5, 1948, Campaign Trips, LCF, box 32.

44. W. H. Lawrence, "Both Candidates Hold They Gained on Tour," *New York Times*, Oct. 3, 1948, Campaign Trips, LCF, box 32.

Chapter 5. The Fall Campaign Continues, October–November 1948

1. "President Truman's 1948 Campaign Speaking Appearances," 1948 Campaign," CVF (1).

2. Alexander H. Uhl, "Truman Starts Tour of Midwest," *Kansas City Star*, Oct. 11, 1948, Campaign Trips, LCF, box 32.

3. Memo, "Appearance of President Truman at Richmond, Wayne County, Indiana, on October 12, 1948," Campaign Speeches and Press Releases, Indiana, Oct. 12 and 13, PSF, box 12.

4. Clayton Knowles, "Truman Starts Tour to Seek Midwest Electoral Votes," *New York Times*, Oct. 11, 1948, Campaign Trips, LCF, box 32.

5. Charter Heslep Letters to Wife, 9-48-3-49, Western Union Press Message, Oct. 11, 1948, CHP, box 2.

6. The October 11 Ohio itinerary was as follows: Cincinnati (breakfast in the Netherlands-Plaza Hotel, 8:35 AM); Hamilton (rear platform, 10:17 AM); Dayton (at Memorial Hall, 11:50 AM); Sidney (rear platform, 1:10 PM); Lima (rear platform, 2:05 PM); Ottowa (rear platform, 2:40 PM); Deshler (rear platform, 3:10 PM); Fostoria (rear platform, 4:05 PM); Willard (rear platform, 4:55 PM); and Rittman (rear platform, 6:30 PM). Quotations that follow are drawn

from PPP, http://www.trumanlibrary.org/publicpapers/index. php?pid=1981&st=&st1.

7. Address at the Armory, Akron, Ohio, Oct. 11, 1948. PPP, http://www. trumanlibrary.org/publicpapers/index.php?pid=1982&st=&st1.

8. Charter Heslep Letters to Wife.

9. Ibid.

10. David McCullough, *Truman*, 691.

11. Ibid., 692–93.

12. Address in Pittsburgh, Pa., Oct. 23, 1948, PPP, http://www.trumanlibrary.org/publicpapers/index.php?pid=2003&st=&st1. For a more complete discussion and analysis of this speech see Ryan, *Harry S. Truman*, 101–105.

13. "Truman: Trying Hard," *Newsweek*, Nov. 1, 1948, Magazine Articles on the President, LCF, box 35.

14. Ferrell. *Harry S. Truman: A Life*, 275.

15. Gardner, *Harry Truman and Civil Rights*, 139. The citation for the Harlem address follows.

16. Address in Harlem, N.Y., Upon Receiving the Franklin Roosevelt Award, Oct. 29, 1948, PPP, http://www.trumanlibrary.org/publicpapers/index.php?pid=2016&st=harlem&st1.

17. Gardner, *Harry Truman and Civil Rights*, 141.

18. Charles S. Murphy Oral History, interviewed by C. T. Morrissey, May 2, 1963.

19. Address at Kiel Auditorium, St. Louis, Mo., Oct. 30, 1948, PPP, http://www.trumanlibrary.org/publicpapers/index.php?pid =2019&st=&st1.

20. Ferrell, *Harry S. Truman: A Life*, 278.

21. Donovan, *Conflict and Crisis*, 431.

22. McCullough, *Truman*, 660.

23. Oct.–Dec., 1948, TCF.

24. Edward T. Folliard, "Truman's Defeat by Wide Margin Seen; 51-Million Vote Expected," *Washington Post*, Nov. 2, 1948, Oct.–Dec., 1948, TCF.

25. Radio Remarks in Independence on Election Eve, Nov. 1, 1948, PPP, http://trumanlibrary.org/publicpapers/index.php?pid=2020&st=&st1.

26. Press Clippings, Marshall Andrews, "Truman Casts Vote, Predicts Victory," *Washington Post,* Nov. 3, 1948, CVF (2).
27. Donaldson, *Truman Defeats Dewey,* 204.
28. "President Truman's 1948 Campaign Speaking Appearances," 1948 Campaign, CVF (1).
29. Rear-Platform Remarks at Vincennes, Ind. (5:10 PM), Nov. 4, 1948, PPP, http://trumanlibrary.org/publicpapers/index.php?pid=2021&st=&st1.
30. Press Clippings, Sam Zagoria, "D.C. Preparing Ceremony and Parade Starting on 11 A.M. Arrival," *Washington Post,* undated (circa Nov. 5, 1948), CVF (2).
31. Remarks upon Arrival at the White House, Washington, D.C., 12:00 PM, Nov. 5, 1948, PPP, http://trumanlibrary.org/publicpapers/index.php?pid=2022&st=&st1.

Chapter 6. Why Truman Won:
The Rhetorical Roots of a Homespun Victory

1. "The Victorious Rebellion of Harry S. Truman," *Newsweek,* Nov. 8, 1948, CVF (2).
2. "Significance," *Newsweek,* Nov. 8, 1948, CVF (2).
3. "The Victorious Rebellion of Harry S. Truman."
4. Newspaper Clippings, Edward A. Harris, "Political Writers, Once United in Saying Dewey Would Win, Stay as One in Telling Why He Didn't," *St. Louis Post-Dispatch,* Nov. 9, 1948, 1948 (2 of 2) Political Files, Clifford Papers, box 20.
5. W. H. Lawrence, "Farmer Vote Cost Dewey Presidency," *New York Times,* Nov. 29, 1948, PRM, Elsey Papers, box 32.
6. W. H. Lawrence, "An Analysis of the Final Election Figures," *New York Times,* Dec. 12, 1948, PRM, Elsey Papers, box 32.
7. Donaldson, *Truman Defeats Dewey,* 187.
8. Ibid, 190.
9. Press Clippings, Joseph C. Goulden, "Give 'em Hell, Harry," *Washington Post,* July 25, 1976, CVF (2).

10. Press Clippings, Anthony Leviero, "The 'Average' American Is Winner of the Election," *New York Times*, Nov. 7, 1948, CVF (4).

11. Press Clippings, H. I. Phillips, "Harry Truman, Solid American," *Kansas City Times*, Nov. 5, 1948, CVF (2).

12. Press Clippings, W. L. White, "Says the People Did It" *Kansas City Times*, Nov. 5, 1948, CVF (2).

13. "By Harry S. Truman: Campaign Barbs that Won Votes . . . by 'Giving Hell' to 'Do-Nothings' and 'G.O. Platitudes,'" *Newsweek*, Nov. 8, 1948, pp. 4–5.

14. Press Clippings, Jay Franklin, "Inside Strategy of the Campaign," *Life*, Nov. 15, 1948, CVF (1).

15. Karabell, *The Last Campaign*, 209.

16. Ayers quoted in Robert H. Ferrell, ed., *Truman in the White House*, 281.

17. Rear Platform Remarks, Shelbyville, Ky., (8:45 AM), Oct. 1, 1948, PPP, http://trumanlibrary.org/publicpapers/index.php?pid=1972 &st=&st1.

18. Press Clippings, Joseph Driscoll, "Reverses and Comebacks Old Story in History of the Truman Family," *St. Louis Post-Dispatch*, Nov. 5, 1948, CVF (2).

19. Rear Platform Remarks, Toledo, Ohio, (11:55 PM), Sept. 6, 1948, PPP, http://trumanlibrary.org/publicpapers/index.php?pid=1797 &st=&st1.

20. Press Clippings, Sam Stavisky, "Career of Truman, Farmer, Soldier, Haberdasher Is Typical of America," *Washington Post*, Nov. 4, 1948, CVF (2).

21. "By Harry S. Truman: Campaign Barbs that Won Votes."

22. Rear Platform Remarks, Auburn, N.Y., 3:21 PM, Oct. 8, 1948, PPP, http://trumanlibrary.org/publicpapers/index.php?pid=1978 &st=&st1.

23. "By Harry S. Truman: Campaign Barbs that Won Votes."

24. Address at the State Fairgrounds, Raleigh, N.C., Oct. 19, 1948, PPP, http://trumanlibrary.org/publicpapers/index.php?pid=1996 &st=&st1.

25. Press Clippings, "Perspective on the Election," editorial, *New York Times,* Nov. 7, 1948, CVF (3).

26. Truman, *Memoirs,* vol. 2, 182.

27. Ibid., 219.

28. McCullough, *Truman,* 655.

29. Rear Platform Remarks, Lock Haven, Pa., (10:25 PM), Oct. 23, 1948, PPP, http://trumanlibrary.org/publicpapers/index.php?pid=2001 &st=&st1.

30. TMF.

31. Cole S. Brembeck, "Harry Truman at the Whistle Stops," *Quarterly Journal of Speech* 48 (1952): 42–50; quotations, 47–48.

32. Hamby, *Man of the People,* 464.

33. Donaldson, *Truman Defeats Dewey,* 178.

34. Brembeck, "Harry Truman at the Whistle Stops," 42.

35. J. Jeffrey Auer, "'Give 'em Hell, Harry!' Harry Truman's Whistle-Stop Campaign," in *Great Speeches for Criticism and Analysis,* 3d ed., ed. Lloyd Rohler and Roger Cook, 23–31; quotation, 30.

Selected Bibliography

Aune, James Arnt, and Enrique D. Rigsby, eds. *Civil Rights Rhetoric and the American Presidency.* College Station: Texas A&M University Press, 2005.

Barber, James D. *The Presidential Character: Predicting Performance in the White House.* 3d ed. Englewood Cliffs, N.J.: Prentice-Hall, 1985.

Berman, William C. *The Politics of Civil Rights in the Truman Administration.* Columbus: Ohio State University Press, 1970.

Borstelmann, Thomas. *The Cold War and the Color Line: American Race Relations in the Global Arena.* Cambridge: Harvard University Press, 2001.

Brembeck, Cole S. "Harry Truman at the Whistle Stops." *Quarterly Journal of Speech* 48 (1952): 42–50.

Clifford, Clark. *Counsel to the President: A Memoir.* New York: Random House, 1991.

Divine, Robert A. "The Cold War and the Election of 1948." *Journal of American History* 59 (1972): 90–110.

Donaldson, Gary A. *Truman Defeats Dewey.* Lexington: The University Press of Kentucky, 1999.

Donovan, Robert J. *Conflict and Crisis: The Presidency of Harry S. Truman, 1945–1948.* New York: W. W. Norton, 1977.

Dudziak, Mary L. *Cold War Civil Rights: Race and the Image of Democracy.* Princeton and Oxford: Princeton University Press, 2000.

Elsey, George M. *An Unplanned Life: A Memoir by George McKee Elsey.* Columbia and London: University of Missouri Press, 2005.

Ferrell, Robert H. *Harry S. Truman: A Life.* Columbia: University of Missouri Press, 1994.

———, ed. *Truman in the White House: The Diary of Eben A. Ayers.* Columbia and London: University of Missouri Press, 1991.

Fields, Wayne. *Union of Words: A History of Presidential Eloquence.* New York: Free Press, 1996.

Gardner, Michael. *Harry Truman and Civil Rights: Moral Courage and Political Risks.* Carbondale and Edwardsville: Southern Illinois University Press, 2002.

Goldzwig, Steven R. "A Social Movement Perspective on Demagoguery: Achieving Symbolic Realignment. *Communication Studies* 40 (1989): 202–28.

Gullan, Harold I. *The Upset that Wasn't: Harry S. Truman and the Crucial Election of 1948.* Chicago: Ivan R. Dee, 1998.

Hamby, Alonzo L. *Man of the People: A Life of Harry S. Truman.* New York: Oxford University Press, 1995.

Hogan, J. Michael, and Glen Williams. "The Rusticity and Religiosity of Huey P. Long." *Rhetoric & Public Affairs* 7 (2004):149–72.

Karabell, Zachary. *The Last Campaign: How Harry Truman Won the 1948 Election.* New York: Alfred A. Knopf, 2000.

Kazin, Michael. *The Populist Persuasion: An American History.* New York: Basic Books, 1995.

Lee, Ronald. "The New Populist Campaign for Economic Democracy: A Rhetorical Exploration." *Quarterly Journal of Speech* 72 (1986): 274–89.

McCoy, Donald R. *The Presidency of Harry S. Truman.* Lawrence: University Press of Kansas, 1984.

McCoy, Donald R., and Richard T. Ruetten, *Quest and Response: Minority Rights and the Truman Administration.* Lawrence: The University Press of Kansas, 1973.

McCullough, David. *Truman.* New York: Simon and Schuster, 1992.

McMath, Jr., Robert C. *American Populism: A Social History, 1877–1898.* New York: Hill and Wang, 1993.

Pauley, Garth. "Harry Truman and the NAACP: A Case Study in Presidential Persuasion on Civil Rights." *Rhetoric & Public Affairs* 2 (1999): 211–41.

———. *The Modern Presidency and Civil Rights.* College Station: Texas A&M University Press, 2001.

Ritter, Kurt, and Martin J. Medhurst, eds. *Presidential Speechwriting:*

From the New Deal to the Reagan Revolution and Beyond. College Station: Texas A&M University Press, 2003.

Rogge, Edward. "The Miracle of '48—Twenty-Six Years in Forming." *Southern Speech Journal* 25 (1960): 264–72.

Rohler, Lloyd. "Conservative Appeals to the People: George Wallace's Populist Rhetoric." *Southern Communication Journal* 64 (1999): 316–22.

Rohler, Lloyd, and Roger Cook, eds. *Great Speeches for Criticism and Analysis.* 3d ed. Greenwood, Ind.: Alistair Press/The Educational Video Group, 1998.

Ross, Irwin. *The Loneliest Campaign: The Truman Victory of 1948.* New York: New American Library, 1968.

Ryan, Halford R. *Harry S. Truman: Presidential Rhetoric.* Westport, Conn., and London: Greenwood Press, 1993.

Skrentny, John David. "The Effect of the Cold War on African American Civil Rights: America and the World Audience, 1945–1968." *Theory and Society* 27 (1998): 237–85.

Truman, Harry S. *Memoirs of Harry S. Truman: Years of Trial and Hope, 1946–1952.* Vol. 2. Garden City, N.Y.: Doubleday, 1956.

Turner, Kathleen, ed. *Doing Rhetorical History: Concepts and Cases.* Tuscaloosa: University of Alabama Press, 1998.

Underhill, Robert. *The Truman Persuasions.* Ames: The Iowa State University Press, 1981.

Index